WHY SOCIALIS˙

Printed by Imprint Digital, Exeter, EX5 5HY
ISBN 978 1 909639 164

Phoenix Press 2016

Phoenix Press
Workers' Liberty
20E Tower Workshops
Riley Road
London, SE1 3DG

ISBN: 978-1-909639-16-4

Contents

Portraits

Cover design by Lizzy Brooks

Published by the Alliance for Workers' Liberty, March 2016
The Alliance for Workers' Liberty is an organisation fighting as part of the labour movement for a socialist alternative to both capitalism and Stalinism, based on common ownership and democracy.
Subscribe to our weekly paper, *Solidarity*, at: www.workersliberty.org/solidarity
www.workersliberty.org • awl@workersliberty.org • 0207 394 8923

WHY SOCIALIST FEMINISM?

The revival of feminist discussion and activity since the late 2000s has drawn many new, younger feminists into writing and organising in Europe and North America. Emerging feminist movements around the world, in India, Turkey, the Middle East and elsewhere, fighting against oppressive political systems and stark economic inequalities, have thrown up new forms of struggle. But what kind of overall feminist perspective do we need to radically change the world?

As revolutionary socialists fighting for a society based on human need not profit, Workers' Liberty makes class struggle and radical social change central to our feminism. We are socialist feminists. This pamphlet explores some of what "socialist feminism" might mean in the context of the latest wave, and current global conditions*.

Carmen Basant argues we revisit the concept of patriarchy to analyse the varietiesof sexism across the world (page 26). Other articles look at current feminist concerns. For instance, Rachael Clarke explores the how feminism which can challenge the sexism that surrounds women's lives and sexualities (page 30).

Articles here argue for fundamental social change and against the conditions that affect us all; it is an alternative to mainstream feminism which focuses only on what individual women can do to improve their situation within the capitalist system. We are against globalised capitalism (Joan Trevor, page 38), in defence of welfare provision (Charlotte Zalens, page 48), for reproductive freedoms (Ellen Trent, page 54) and the struggle against oppressive religious institutions (Elizabeth Butterworth, page 64).

We understand feminism to be a public political movement which arose inside bourgeois societies, varying in its scope and political complexion, across geography and history. Awakened by the promise of equality set out by bourgeois democratic politics, women began to organise for their rights, to be considered citizens, human beings of equal worth. Through continuous struggles women around the world have won many rights — the right to vote, to divorce, to own and dispose of property, to have an education. And yet in many parts of the world women still do not have those rights. Moreover, in those parts of the world where those rights have been won, women are still beaten up by their partners, are sacked when they are pregnant, are sexually harassment on public transport and do on.

Socialists do not think the continuation of women's oppression is the result of an "patriarchal culture" which is *unvarying* across space and time. We know women's oppression is thousands of years old but the mechanisms of our oppression have changed. And we can differentiate between how women are oppressed in, for instance, India and the UK. Nor do we see sexist attitudes as something that are "natural" or innate in men or, at best, almost impossible to shift, as many "radical feminists" would argue. Ultimately our oppression is rooted in the material facts

---

* *The Case for Socialist Feminism,* published in 1986, dealt with debates in the women's movement at the end of the "second wave". It can be downloaded:
womensfightback.wordpress.com/resources/the-case-for-socialist-feminism/

of class society, and for most women in the world the particular forms of modern class society, capitalism. A combination of political struggle and a fight to change material conditions can change women's lives and shift sexist attitudes.

In the second wave feminist movement socialist and Marxist feminists tried to develop ideas about how oppression works by rethinking Marxism. That kind of work is to a limited extent being revisited by anti-capitalist feminists. A fully-integrated analysis of oppression(s) has been the focus for academic and some activist feminists, asking questions about how race, gender and other oppressions as well as class exploitation work together?

This pamphlet is our engagement with some of the theoretical debates; there are articles here on social reproduction (Rachael Clarke, page 5), intersectionality (Ellen Trent, page 17).

Finally we republish two articles which describe the longer tradition we stand within. Jessica Bradwell writes about the German Social Democratic women's movement (page 69) and Jayne Evans explains the role of women's socialist activism in the Russian revolution (page 82).

The dominance of "liberal feminism", which sees solutions for individual women as key to change, is somewhat accounted for by the decline in Marxist ideas in feminism. On one level this isn't surprising — despite the rise of dramatic social movements across the globe, the organised working class remains a marginal force in most struggles. Historical and contemporary examples of the potential of social change, once working-class women and men organise together in strikes, in working-class communities, remain obscure to many activists.

We see this pamphlet as a starting point for a debate with other feminists, socialists and anti-capitalists. We realise that it is not a comprehensive overview of socialist feminism, or, indeed, of some of our own discussions (e.g. issues of gender identity, or the pre-capitalist origins of women's oppression). We hope to publish critiques, responses and further thoughts on different topics in a future edition.

Please get in touch if you would like to discuss, disagree with, or debate these ideas.

CAPITALISM AND WOMEN'S OPRESSION

BY RACHAEL CLARK

Women in the UK still do more housework than men. The domestic tasks of an advanced capitalist country like the UK, such as cooking, cleaning and caring, are still naturalised as "women's work". The domination of women's lives by domestic labour has no basis in biology or nature; the role that women perform in childrearing occupies a relatively short period of our lives. Yet the idea that "a woman's place is in the home" still influences the roles we take on in our domestic lives and in the labour market. It shapes the kind of jobs we do, the hours we work and the discrimination we face in the workplace. It underpins sexism in all aspects of life.

To give a brief history, the "sexual division of labour", the rough allocation of domestic work (cooking and childrearing) to women and productive work (making things, sometimes for sale) to men, is older than capitalism. In *The Case for Socialist Feminism*[1] Workers' Liberty noted that women in the precapitalist, patriarchal household were "domestic slaves". We noted that in feudal Western Europe, where the household was the centre of much economic activity, "the sexual division of labour was not rigid" and that women's oppression was probably "the least harsh" of all precapitalist civilisations. Yet, we added, women's "economic activity was much more centred on the home than men's"; women lacked economic independence, and the "household headed by the father was the norm".

As capitalism became established, the sexual division of labour and the inequality that it reproduced was institutionalised in a new way. Economic production moved from the home to specialised work-sites, such as workshops and factories. For the first time, domestic work was almost completely isolated from production; it became a separate sphere — although women and children continued to do "homeworking", for low or piecework wages.

The division of labour according to sex survived the transition from precapitalist to capitalist society. That it has remained "relatively invariant across successive modes of production" might lead us to conclude that domestic labour is assigned to us by a timeless, unconquerable force. Indeed, the idea that our roles in production are shaped by "timeless relations between the sexes" has led some feminists to conclude that society's "fundamental characteristic" is "patriarchal" rather than "capitalist" (a view criticised here: S Himmelweit and S Mohun, *Domestic Labour and Capital*).

However, we can see from the brief history above that domestic labour and its relation to production is not timeless; it has varied across economic systems. Today, capitalism is the dominant global economic system and women's role in domestic work is one of the structures that underpins women's oppression in this society. If

---

1. Available to download here:
womensfightback.wordpress.com/resources/the-case-for-socialist-feminism/

we are to rid ourselves of oppression, we must look at how domestic work relates to the capitalist system; we can then understand what demands we can put forward and what struggles we can wage.

Lise Vogel's *Marxism and the Oppression of Women: Toward a Unitary Theory* (first published in 1986 and reprinted in 2013) provides us with a framework with which to understand how capitalism, domestic work and women's oppression relate.

Vogel explains that, for capitalism, like "all societies characterised by exploitation", "an essential condition for production is the... renewal of a subordinated class of direct producers (i.e. workers) committed to the labour process".

Workers are "the bearers of labour power". Labour power means our ability to work, which under capitalism becomes a commodity; workers exchange their labour power for a wage from the capitalist. Capitalists use labour power to make commodities and other kinds of goods, which they sell to generate a surplus (a profit). Without labour power, there can be no surplus, no profit. Without surplus, capitalism cannot reproduce itself (buy more labour, make more goods, create more surplus). Capitalism is only sustained because the capitalist class calls all the shots — controls the conditions under which people have to sell their labour power in order to survive. This cycle is called capitalist accumulation.

For Vogel, the process of the reproduction of labour power is important. It is a "condition of existence for capital", it is a link in the chain of capitalist accumulation. Hence Vogel highlights the reproduction of labour power as a crucial aspect of domestic labour.

The process of the reproduction of labour power comprises both the day-to-day feeding, washing and clothing ("maintenance") of workers and bringing new workers into the world ("generational replacement").

SOCIAL REPRODUCTION PERSPECTIVE

Vogel describes her framework for linking up domestic work, capitalist accumulation and women's oppression as a "social reproduction perspective". Her aim is to establish the ways in which women's oppression is integral to capitalist relations. According to this perspective "women's oppression has its roots in women's differential location within social reproduction as a whole".

Vogel says this perspective can be found in Marx's writings, but that it has to be expanded upon. Marx described the "reproduction of the conditions of production", the processes that enable a society to perpetuate. For example, under feudalism, Marx said, a serf had to produce enough "to reproduce his conditions of labour in addition to his subsistence"; every mode of production, he continued, must include the "reproduction of its own operating conditions". Applying this concept to capitalism, Vogel argues that "social reproduction requires... a supply of labour power.... to set the labour process in motion". The reproduction of labour power is one element of capitalist social reproduction. For Vogel, domestic labour's role in reproducing labour power is the link between domestic labour and social reproduction.

The social reproduction perspective is a critique of the "dualist" logic used by some socialist-feminists (e.g. Heidi Hartmann) who analysed women's oppression as a result of two separate structures, capitalism and patriarchy. It is also a critique of a similar "dual systems perspective" in much socialist analysis of women's oppression, which essentially characterised class and sex oppression as "autonomous phenomena" and bolted "the so-called woman question" onto class analysis.

Vogel aims to integrate the mechanics of women's oppression firmly within capitalist relations. She looks at the "level of total social reproduction", at women's situation within the social system. So when Vogel talks about the importance of domestic work, she is not talking about work performed within individual families; she is concerned with the systemic level at which "the totality of labourers....is maintained and replaced". Similarly, her concept of women's oppression is not one of male dominance on an individual level or within working class households. Ferguson and McNally explain her conception here in the introduction to the 2013 edition:

"While the family is fundamental to women's oppression in capitalist society, the pivot of this oppression is not women's domestic labour for men or children... Rather, it pivots on the social significance of domestic labour for capital."

The role of supplying labour power shapes the relationship between the working-class household and capitalist production. But why are women specifically oppressed? Vogel's answer is that women's role in "generational replacement" is crucial: "women's oppression in class societies is rooted in their differential position with respect to generational replacement processes".

Women get pregnant and give birth; men don't. This assigns women the task of

ELEANOR MARX (1855-1898)

Eleanor Marx was a political activist from a young age. Aged 10 she wrote long letters to Abraham Lincoln critiquing his handling of the US Civil War; aged 12 she developed a passionate interest in Ireland; and at 16 she visited the Paris Commune.

Marx joined the Social Democratic Federation in the early 1880s and when it split she helped formed the Socialist League — growing into a dedicated fighter for socialism and women's liberation. She was an active strike organiser and member of the executive of the Gas Workers and General Labours' Union, working with unskilled workers of the East End of London, including women's branches. She was one of the foremost fighters in the British labour movement for the cause of working-class socialist internationalism.

Marx was a strong supporter of the women's suffrage movement but believed working-class women needed to organise independently — re-titling the so-called "woman question" the "working-woman question". She wrote on international class struggle, literature and poetry and feminism.

In *The Woman Question* (1886), Marx criticised the judgement of women's sexuality and relationships and argued for comprehensive sex education.

reproducing new generations of workers. Vogel says, "biological differences constitute the material precondition for the social construction of gender differences." The oppression that accompanies women's reproductive role "originates as a historical legacy from oppressive divisions of labour in earlier class societies."

In summary, Vogel sets out a useful framework, which makes the links between domestic labour, capitalism, reproduction of labour power, social reproduction and women's oppression. Its real strength is that it does not present these relationships as fixed. Capitalism is not presented as an unshifting monolith that will ensnare women eternally to the domestic sphere. Vogel presents capitalism and women's relationship to it as susceptible to change, from capitalism's contradictory drives, the pressure of class struggle and the pressure of battles for equality at all levels of society.

CAPITAL'S CONTRADICTIONS

Capitalism does not stand still. Its in-built drive to accumulate promotes expansion and intensification of production; this motivates capitalists to expand production, under their control, setting up new factories and warehouses, building offices and infrastructure. Meanwhile, capitalism, says Vogel, designates specialised sites for the reproduction of labour power, of which "working class families located in private households represent the dominant form". Thus capitalism instigates the "spatial, temporal and institutional separation between domestic labour and the capitalist production process". The split between the public and private, the productive and reproductive, and the waged and unwaged spheres is entrenched to a greater extent than under any previous economic system.

Vogel notes that this demarcation of spheres "forms the basis for a series of powerful ideological structures which develop a forceful life of their own". However, Vogel insists that this ideology, such as the split between public/private realms that exists under capitalism, is far from timeless: it is "rooted in the economic workings of the capitalist mode of production".

But there is an important contradictory tendency. While demanding a supply of labour power and appearing to entrench the domestic sphere, capital simultaneously undermines it. The capitalist drive to accumulate pushes women into waged labour; this has been increasing since the 1950s and continues to increase. In the UK by 1996, 67% of married or cohabiting mothers with dependent children were in work and by 2013 this had increased to 72%.

Therefore, we can observe what Vogel describes as capitalism's "tendency to decrease the amount of work performed in each household". Notwithstanding barriers, such as the cost of childcare provision and the "basic physiological process of childrearing", there have been real overall reductions in women's domestic labour. This has been realised through domestic technology, such as washing machines, or through socialisation either by capitalism or the state in the form of healthcare, education, childcare, or supermarket-bought groceries.

The drive for capitalist accumulation produces a second tendency that pulls women away from domestic labour and into waged labour. Vogel calls this tendency "the equalisation of labour force participation". Capital is mobile, Vogel explains. It moves to wherever it can yield most profit. It therefore requires labour power that can be flexible, that can move between industries and, in Marx's words, "from one local centre of production to another". To some extent, it wants women to engage in production without domestic labour forming a barrier.

Women are caught between capitalism's two contradictory requirements: "increased female labour-force participation" and the "capacity to perform domestic labour". Vogel comments: "As those primarily responsible for domestic labour, women contribute heavily to the maintenance and renewal" of the working class, including wage workers and those "who do not or cannot themselves enter wage-labour" (e.g. the disabled and the elderly). She continues: "To the extent, however, that women enter wage labour they become less able to take care of members of the household not presently in the work force". Does capital want women to go to work or stay at home? The short answers is, it wants both, to one degree or another depending on circumstances.

Capitalism attempts to resolve the contradiction according to its requirements. For example, if a certain industry in a location which employs women expands (e.g., the tourist industry, including hotels, bars and restaurants) the local state might step in to help look after the elderly or organise childcare. But, equally likely, working women will juggle domestic caring responsibilities with waged work. That's how the contradictory roles that women perform in relation to capitalism get resolved!

Vogel notes that the contradiction over whether to pull women in or out of the labour market partly reflects contradictions between capital's long-term and short-term interests. Vogel also describes the reduction of domestic labour as "no more than a general trend". She stresses that the "history of a particular society" and the "class conflict within it" have an effect on the outcomes.

Vogel provides a few speculative examples of ways that capitalism might develop different priorities, and provide for its contradictory requirements, reproduction of labour power and productive labour and most of these have, in fact, come to pass. If capital has a ready supply of new labour, e.g., migrant labour from outside, there will be less pressure on working class women to produce the next generation of workers; the sex division of labour may therefore be weak and women and men may work alongside each other in the same jobs. If capital needs to maximise its productivity, it could push both men and women into low paid work, as it did in the mid-19th century, which caused upheaval in traditional family structures. Capitalism may want to seize on the advantages of women's participation in the labour force, but also have concerns about the long-term reproduction of labour power; it may require the state to organise massive intervention into some aspects of social reproduction, e.g. care for children and older people.

Arguably, because in the advanced capitalist world women are a permanent part of the labour force, the nature of this contradictory situation is undergoing fundamental change. A full assessment of that situation needs a lot of empirical research. We can make only a few comments based on recent statistics:

1. Domestic responsibilities still restrict women's participation in the labour market. While it is significant that more working age women than ever are now in paid work, it is also notable that 42% are part-time. Despite the general increase in the number of women in work, "the percentage of women doing a part time role has fluctuated between 42 and 45% over the last 30 years". (Office of National

Statistics, *Women in the Labour Market*, September 2013). Women and men's employment rates remain roughly similar until age 28, which is the average age for a woman to give birth to her first child. Above 28, men consistently have a higher employment rate; the gap narrows in older age when women re-join the workforce once children have grown up (ONS).

Women's economic "inactivity" has fallen overall, but it remains higher than that of men. The "Gender Jobs Split", a report on young people in the labour market, notes that this reflects "a continued divide in terms of responsibilities for unpaid care giving. Young women are more likely to do unpaid care work (including responsibilities for siblings, dependent children and relatives), and this will contribute to lower employment rates amongst young women."

Childcare provision does not adequately meet the needs of women who wish to work. Childcare costs went up by a third in the five years preceding 2015, according to The Family and Childcare Trust; the cost for the average family has soared by £1,500 a year since 2010. The expense of childcare is pushing some women out of paid work; 20% of mothers in work would like to work more hours but say it is financially unviable. Employer-provided childcare is usually limited to costly "salary sacrifice schemes", which deduct childcare costs directly from wages. To obviate the expense, there has been increased reliance on "informal care" provided by family members, most of whom are female, which reinforces the restriction that domestic responsibility places on women's participation in waged work. The 2015 Conservative government is on paper committed to "giving more people the opportunity to get into work", with the promise of increasing free childcare from 15 to 30 hours a week for three and four year olds.

2. The labour market remains segregated along gender lines, with women dominating in jobs that mirror the unpaid work that women traditionally performed in the home. For example, 82% of workers in "caring, leisure and other services" are women, whereas 10% of workers in "skilled trades" are women (ONS, *Women in the Labour Market*).

Low pay is prevalent in the sectors of the labour market in which women dominate. TUC Policy Officer Sally Brett commented in March 2015:

"Three in five National Minimum Wage jobs are held by women, two in five by men. Over a quarter of women (27 per cent) earn less than the Living Wage; fewer than one in six men do (16 per cent). For women working part time, which two-fifths of women do, the incidence of low pay is even higher — two in five earn less than the Living Wage and in some parts of the country most part-time women do not earn enough to give them a decent standard of living" (leftfootforward.org, March 2015).

Women's jobs pay poorly because they are devalued as "women's work". Many women juggle care commitments with work, which restricts women from seeking alternative employment with higher pay; this helps to entrench low pay in sectors dominated by women.

In March 2015, the TUC reported a record number of women in work, but emphasised that since the financial crisis, "most of the net growth in women's employment has been in low-skilled and low-paying sectors". House of Commons Library figures reveal that, since 2010, nearly 60% of new jobs for women were in low-paying sectors, compared with 39% of new jobs for men.

Successive governments have cut out-of-work benefits to push parents into low paid work. Lone parents with children could at one time claim Income Support until children were 12; this was lowered to seven, then to five years old. Since 2014, single parents with a child who is aged one or over must attend work-focussed interviews and face benefit cuts as sanctions if they do not engage in work-related activity. This has been accompanied by real-terms cuts in Child Benefit. In addition, the 2010-15 government capped benefits at £500 per week for a couple or lone parent, irrespective of the number of children in the household.

From 2001, Child Tax Credit and Working Tax Credit were used as an incentive to encourage parents into the low-waged labour market. They were paid primarily to working families to supplement low incomes and assist with childcare costs. In 2015, the Conservative government announced large cuts to tax credits but was forced to retreat.

From this picture, it appears that capital is meeting its requirements for labour force participation and benefiting from women's work in low paid jobs. For a while, Working Tax Credits were used to actively encourage women into the low-waged labour market and, whatever happens in the future with the benefit, women will continue in low paid work because cuts to out-of-work benefits, the gender segregation of the labour market and care commitments leave women with few alternatives.

The high proportion of part-time women workers indicates that capital is simultaneously meeting its requirements for labour power renewal through informal care and women's unpaid work in the home. This diminishes the priority governments give to providing free — or even affordable — childcare. The Conservatives' plan to offer 30 hours a week free childcare is more about encouraging women to engage in low paid work than it is about removing the barrier of domestic responsibility that prohibits women from participating in the labour market on an equal footing with men.

But capital still wants two things from women: our productive and our reproductive abilities. This means that although it appears to be getting both at a cheap price at the moment, there remains potential in this framework for class struggle to balance this contradiction in a manner more favourable to us. For example, the drive to accumulate means capital needs workers of all genders; through class struggle we can therefore fight to level up our conditions, eroding the second-class character of segregated "women's work".

As already stated, Vogel believes oppression arises from women's reproductive function within capitalism as an overall system. Therefore, although Vogel, like other feminists, identifies that domestic labour plays a role in producing women's oppression, she does not imagine that the struggle for women's liberation will be confined to the reproductive sphere. For her, the sphere of production is the prime site for class struggle:

"The social reproduction perspective starts out from a theoretical position — namely that class struggle over the conditions of production represents the central dynamic of social development in societies characterised by exploitation."

Vogel has demonstrated to us that the productive and reproductive spheres are both integral to the capitalist system. She asserts that class struggle, primarily in the productive sphere, is the lever that can shift exploitative and oppressive relations. However, it has to be a certain kind of class struggle, one which pays attention to women's situation. What class struggle can we wage and what demands can we raise to challenge the structures of women's oppression? Here are some suggestions.

1. Raise women workers' pay; break down the gender segregation of the workforce. Vogel comments that factors such as capital's need for "different categories of workers" and "ideological hegemony over a divided working class" conflict against its long-term demand for a mobile, flexible workforce. On the one hand, the need to divide is strong and continues to play an important role in determining the extent to which "women remain segregated within and without the workforce". On the other hand, in a sense, the capitalist labour market is an equaliser: all workers present as equals to exchange their labour power for a wage; we are all exploitable equals. Women workers in low-waged "women's work" can use capitalism's logic of equality as grounds for their struggle to level up conditions and challenge unequal pay. Women can also battle against discrimination and sexism in traditionally male, higher-paid, skilled working-class jobs, such as engineering.

Too often, women's low wages make it financially unviable for women to work while men stay at home. If men and women earned the same, it would make equal financial sense for either gender to do the caring. That would undo some of the material and ideological strings that tie women to the domestic sphere.

Though the struggle of workers to be equal in our exploitation is not a revolutionary struggle, it can undermine the material inequality that underpins the ideology of women's inferiority, contributes to our political isolation and undermines attempts to organise.

2. Break down barriers to women's participation in the labour force.

Alongside the second class character of "women's work", the extent of our workforce participation is still a factor in our oppression.

Our part-time or non-participation in the labour force, partly resulting from domestic roles, produces individual poverty during our working lives and retirement. It denies women the economic independence that comes with earning a full-time wage, which is a progressive consequence of the advent of capitalism.

While we argue that men and women should share domestic work, we *acknowledge* that, in the immediate term, tradition and the physiological process of child-birth will make it hard to completely shift age-old gender roles. Therefore, we need to place demands on employers and governments to implement measures that avert discrimination and remove barriers to women's employment. For example, we should possess the legal right to be granted, not just to request, "flexible working". The USA provides a stark example of the barriers still encountered by women; most states and employers do not provide maternity leave, which harms the health of women who cannot afford adequate time off to recover from childbirth.

It is possible for us to maximise on the fact that capital simultaneously needs our labour power and our ability to reproduce it. We can pressure the state to provide services that alleviate the burden of domestic work, such as childcare. Of course, capitalists will wish to provide these measures on their terms so that we slot into the existing labour market. However, to demand state-funded, high quality childcare, flexible to our needs and the needs of children, is more than acquiescence to the needs of capitalist exploitation. It is a way to enable greater economic independence through waged work, to promote equality within our

THE FORD DAGENHAM STRIKE

The 1968 strike for re-grading and equal pay organised by women sewing machinists at Ford Dagenham is one of the heroic episodes of British labour movement history. In terms of both working-class militancy and women's self-assertiveness, it was an important catalyst for further struggles and gains in the period that followed.

The machinists originally called for their jobs to be re-graded from unskilled to semi-skilled, but it soon became clear that a big underlying problem was the existence of a "women's rate" which was only 85% of even the unskilled men's rate. Equal pay became one of the strikers' key demands, and their action galvanised wider struggles.

The women weren't just fighting against sexism in wider society and law; they were also fighting for recognition by their own unions. Lower pay for women was, at base, a way of capitalists saving money — this both generated and was reinforced by institutionalised ideas that their work was less important and their wages "pocket money" to support their "serious duties" in the home. Since the 19th century, women workers had been viewed by sections of the movement as a threat to men's employment, and some trade unions had supported bans on married women working.

The National Joint Action Campaign Committee for Women's Equal Rights was formed by women trade unionists, organising a 1,000 strong demonstration for equal pay in 1969. The 1970 Equal Pay Act armed women with the right to demand equal pay with men doing "like work", but it wasn't the end of the story. The 1970s saw other equal pay strikes, the most famous of which was the 1976 Trico strike, at a Brentford factory making windscreen wipers. Women are still fighting for equal pay today — it remains just as important as ever that we remember Dagenham and other struggles of the late 60s and 70s and learn the lessons.

class, to cohere the working class as a force capable of overturning class relations. It also addresses the governmental realm of struggle, asserting a claim for a state that provides services to meet our needs, and which are under our democratic control.

3. A shorter working week. We should not restrict our aspirations to women, or men, spending more time at work! We aspire to work less.

The demand for a shorter working week has long been a demand of the working-class movement because it cuts against capital's core motivation: to accumulate by making us work the requisite number of hours it needs to make profit. The easiest and crudest method that capital has traditionally employed to enhance accumulation is to extend the time we spend at work, which had brutal consequences for workers in 19th-century Britain. Even today, the demand for a shorter working week remains a challenge to capital's attempt to subsume every hour of our existence to the dictates of accumulation; it is a challenge to capital's absolute control of the production process; it is a claim for working-class control over life.

The demand for more time away from work would free up time for domestic life. Men should not wait for shorter working hours before taking on an equal share of domestic tasks, just as many women today do not have the luxury of short working hours when carrying out the lion's share of housework. But more time at home would ease equal participation in domestic labour.

It might seem strange to demand state provision, such as childcare, to reduce domestic labour, while simultaneously demanding more time away from work to do domestic labour ourselves. But it is not so strange when we consider that, unlike the products of capitalist production, which belong 100% to the capitalist, the products of domestic labour — our children and the homes that we make and look after — do not belong to capital. To call for women to be cut off from domestic labour entirely would not be wholly desirable or necessary. Surely it is more desirable to call for more time at the expense of capital to enable both genders to do more of the aspects of domestic labour that we enjoy, such as spending time with our children? This does not contradict demanding high quality childcare, and working out how certain aspects of domestic work, such as washing clothing and shopping, could be socialised and organised by communities.

YANAR MOHAMMED (1960-)

Is director of the Organization for Women's Freedom in Iraq (OWFI) and an active socialist feminist in Iraq. She is a trained architect and lived in Canada in the 1990s. There she became politically active in the Worker-communist Party of Iraq and a campaign called Defence of Iraqi Women's Rights. In 2003, after the US/UK invasion which toppled Saddam Hussein, Yanar Mohammed and other socialist feminists re-established the campaign as the OWFI in Baghdad. The OWFI has set up women's shelters and safe houses to protect women threatened by domestic abuse, so-called "honour" killings, and trafficking of young women. They have exposed prison conditions for women in Iraq. Most recently Yanar has campaigned against the oppression of women by Daesh (Islamic State).

MOVE BEYOND DOMESTIC LABOUR

It is the subordination of our reproductive function to the requirements of capital, not the process of reproduction itself, which creates women's structural oppression. Similarly, it is not productive labour, but our lack of our control over the capitalist labour process, which produces exploitation. A liberated society would need to continue the processes involved in production.

Vogel helps us understand that separate productive and domestic spheres do not exist as a result of any inherent quality in the tasks involved in productive or reproductive labour. The spheres arise because, under capitalism, production is for the purpose of profit, rather than human need, and necessitates the organisation of labour into distinct spheres to pursue this goal. Vogel argues that in societies not characterised by class exploitation there would be no need for a distinction between "productive" labour and "reproductive" labour. The processes of producing things and of the tasks required to reproduce ourselves would be integrated, meshed together and in a collective enterprise to satisfy all of society's needs. The distinction between the two spheres, alongside exploitation and the oppression arising from women's structural function for capital would all, in Friedrich Engels' phrase, "wither away".

This might sound utopian, or too similar to the idea that "come the revolution" women's oppression will automatically disappear. But it is important to note that Vogel admits that her framework is not intended as a "full-blown exposition of women's oppression" in all its aspects and forms of society. What she provides is an effective illustration of the degree to which class and gender oppression are integrated in today's dominant economic system, capitalism. Her conclusion, that class society, the domestic/productive distinction and women's oppression, are so integrated that it is possible to conceive of these elements withering away together, is an expression of the framework of integrated oppression that she has articulated.

THE WORKING-CLASS FAMILY

Vogel situates the working-class family as integral to capitalism; she describes it as "a kin-based site for the reproduction of labour power". To Vogel, the family is the most common form for carrying out this function; its function is more important than its form. She sums this up: "It is responsibility for the domestic labour necessary to capitalist social reproduction — and not the sex division of labour or the family per se — that materially underpins the perpetuation of women's oppression".

Vogel criticises the "Wages for Housework" tradition, which among other things seeks to draw attention to women's domestic labour, partly on the grounds that it separates out and therefore entrenches the domestic sphere. She also declares the demand to abolish the family to be "utopian". It is one thing to note that women's entry into wage-labour has transformed and in some ways eroded family structures. It is another to call for the abolition of the family as an end in itself.

Vogel argues it is better to reduce and redistribute domestic labour in the course of transforming it into an integral component of social production, thereby undermining the foundation of the oppression of women within the individual household and society.

CONCLUSION

Vogel's framework does not seek to explain the breadth of women's oppression. However, it illustrates some of the ways in which class and gender oppression are integrated in capitalist relations. Vogel relates gender oppression to the workings of capitalism through her insight that oppression arises from women's reproduction of labour power; this is seen as part of the process of capitalist social reproduction. Vogel's perspective sees domestic work, capitalist production and social reproduction as part of an integrated, shifting whole, which opens up the prospect for us to struggle in the productive and reproductive spheres to challenge these relations. Vogel's framework encourages us to raise demands that seek to erode the gender divisions within the working class, just as we seek to erode the distinction between the productive and domestic spheres. This framework promotes an approach that works towards cohering our class into a force that is united because it is equal, which is capable of overhauling the gender oppression that is entwined within class relations.

movement. But this meant making "personal" problems into issues for collective action; telling women that their problems were not just a matter of personal inadequacies, but part of a social oppression directed against all women; and enlarging socialist ideas with a wider humanism. Experience was important, but not an end point for understanding the world. We have to complement our experience with study of history and the systematic, structural causes of oppression as well as discussion with others.

A key problem with a politics based simply on identity is its relationship to "difference". Perhaps ironically, identity politics fails to recognise diversity of experience and ideas and creates difference and division where they don't really exist.

Even an intersectional approach which recognises the variety of identities in a given group and seeks unity in struggle, fails to address the problem that not all people who identify in a particular way think the same, see problems in the same way, want to struggle in the same way, or are right about what is best for that group of people. There are plenty of women who have experienced the world at the "intersections of oppression" but have taken an individualist or even right-wing approach to tackling that. Their experience has not led them to believe society must be radically transformed.

SOJOURNER TRUTH (C.1797-1883)

Sojourner Truth was an African-American abolitionist and women's rights activist. Born into slavery, Truth escaped with her baby daughter in 1826 and became the first black woman to win a case to recover her son from a white man.

In 1840, the World Anti-Slavery Convention was held in London; but women delegates were kept out. In response, women set up Female Anti-Slavery Societies in America. There was common ground between feminism and anti-slavery (abolitionism): a shared cause of rights and emancipation.

But not everyone saw this link. In 1851, Truth attended a women's convention in Akron, Ohio. Some of the women present did not want her to speak, because they did not want the feminist movement associated with abolitionism. But Truth did speak and challenged the exclusion of black women from the convention in her famous speech "Ain't I a woman?"

"That man over there says that women need to be helped into carriages, and lifted over ditches, and to have the best place everywhere. Nobody ever helps me into carriages, or over mud-puddles, or gives me any best place! And ain't I a woman? Look at me! Look at my arm! I have ploughed and planted, and gathered into barns, and no man could head me! And ain't I a woman? I could work as much and eat as much as a man — when I could get it — and bear the lash as well! And ain't I a woman? I have borne thirteen children, and seen them most all sold off into slavery, and when I cried out with my mother's grief, none but Jesus heard me! And ain't I a woman?"

On the other hand, identity politics remains a politics of difference, focusing on the differences between groups. Even when not essentialist, identity politics sees our identities as fixed and static. It ignores that we are complex and multi-sided and capable of being much more than our existing identities. Our identity, and our experience of it, is not organised in discrete categories which are more or less important at different points or "intersections".

Part of what makes our experience of oppression and discrimination depressing and aggravating is that the discrimination puts us in a box and treats us accordingly — it denies our identity as a whole and complex human being. To challenge oppression it is important that we see ourselves as both a combination of particular identities and as more than the sum of those parts, as human beings. A humanistic approach is vital for feminism which has to appeal against the "natural" order of women's subordination; to appeal against sexist dehumanisation of women; and to appeal to a principle of treating every human being equally.

Recognising each other as human beings as well as members of particular groups allows for the recognition that we have shared interests as well as self/group interests and through this for the generation of solidarity. Our struggles must be shaped by this if we are to create a world where identity can both be transcended and set free. Solidarity stands in opposition to the dog-eat-dog principles of capitalism and class society — it points the way to, and makes possible, a more equal, fair and human world.

The further problem with intersectionality, for the most part, though not always, is not that it ignores class but that class is seen as another ideology of oppression. Intersectionality gives "capitalism" and "class" looser definitions: capitalism as social, cultural, political and economic relations, and class as a cultural construct, defined through the lens of identity and experience.

INTERSECTIONALITY, IDENTITY AND CLASS

A class analysis is crucial to understanding the roots and development of oppression. It helps us understand that, although often embodied in individual relations, oppression is born of structures within society. By analysing the economic and social roots of oppression in history and society we can see that it is not natural or absolute — this is important in realising that we can challenge and change it too.

For Marxists, definitions of class in terms of privilege, culture, income, etc. are

CHEN BILAN (1902-1987)

Joined the League of Socialist Youth in 1922 and the Chinese Communist Party in 1923. She studied in Moscow in 1924-25, returned to China and was active as a Marxist in the Chinese women's movement and labour movement in the late 1920s. Chen Bilan became a Trotskyist and worked with Chen Duxiu, Peng Shuzhi and others from 1929. She left China in 1948 just before the Maoists came to power, working for the post-Trotsky Fourth International while in exile in Hong Kong, Vietnam, France and the United States.

far from irrelevant — they can help explain real and important divisions within the working class as we understand it. But they are not adequate.

Our definition is not a matter of preference, but of looking at the world around us and explaining its dynamics. Class is a matter of the social relationships which drive capitalism — the mechanisms through which the ruling minority pump wealth out of the majority who do the work. This is what we mean by "exploitation", as distinct from "oppression". Under capitalism, the majority of the population, in order to live, must sell their labour power (ability to work) to an individual or institution in possession of means of producing wealth (material goods, services, etc., in the form of commodities), in exchange for a wage. In most cases, and certainly across the working class, wages are less than the value of commodities produced; this is where capitalist profit or surplus value comes from. This relationship of exploitation creates or constitutes both capital and the working class.

Capitalists care about the divisions of ethnicity, gender, culture, nation etc., among workers because, on the one hand, they provide the basis for extra exploitation of some groups, and, on the other, they undermine working-class solidarity and resistance. However, despite this there remains a real basis for solidarity — the common experience of capitalist exploitation.

A Marxist definition of class shows how socialism is more than just a good, or utopian, idea. Class exploitation is not necessarily worse or more fundamental than other oppressions; but because the class structure is bound up with nature, technology and how society's wealth is produced, it is a powerful force in shaping oppression. The wage-labour system of exploitation endows capital with enormous wealth and enormous power — including far greater self-consciousness and self-confidence than its class victim. But it also puts workers in a position to organise, struggle and develop their consciousness so that they can begin to act as a class fighting for themselves. More than that, such movements, at a high enough pitch, can develop a dynamic which points beyond the limits of capitalism, to a new society based on solidarity.

Overthrowing class exploitation is a necessary building block, but not enough in itself, to abolish oppression. Socialism will not immediately end all oppression, but the roots of oppression lie in class society — by overthrowing class society and cutting the roots of oppression we can create the conditions for liberation. In a society based on democracy and solidarity it will be possible to work to end all forms of oppression and exploitation.

So understanding class in a Marxist sense shows not just that the world can be changed, but how to change it. That is why Marxist politics is fundamentally "about" the working class, in all its incredible diversity.

PRIVILEGE THEORY

Privilege theory originated among American academics in the same era as intersectionality, and is popular now in UK student politics and academia. There is a big overlap but it is not the same thing as intersectionality. However, many privilege theorists use intersectionality to explain how people can be "privileged" in some areas and face oppression in others.

Privilege theory holds that oppression is created and recreated through other people having unearned advantages, or privileges — for example, men are privileged in not experiencing sexism, white people are privileged in not experiencing racism and so on.

Peggy McIntosh famously described privilege as an "invisible knapsack":

"I have come to see white privilege as an invisible package of unearned assets that I can count on cashing in each day, but about which I was 'meant' to remain oblivious. White privilege is like an invisible weightless knapsack of special provisions, assurances, tools, maps, guides, codebooks, passports, visas, clothes, compass, emergency gear, and blank checks" (McIntosh, *White Privilege and Male Privilege*).

If intersectionality is an understanding of the way that oppressions intersect, privilege is an understanding of what causes those oppressions:

"The conditions I have described here work to systematically overempower certain groups. Such privilege simply confers dominance, gives permission to control, because of one's race or sex." (McIntosh, *White Privilege and Male Privilege*)

Again, although we recognise that oppression lives in inter-personal relationships, privilege theory ignores or sets aside the structural roots of oppression. In expressing the unconscious nature of privilege, it is pessimistic about the possibility of overcoming it. The best that can be hoped for is increased self-awareness and the mitigation, or "checking", of privilege on an individual basis.

Privilege theory sees society like a "see-saw" and offers a levelling out solution — "you're up there because I'm down here… so, you need to come down so I can go up" ("check your privilege"). In contrast, through fighting for a radical transformation of society in which the people who produce the wealth, the working-class, take power and use society's wealth for the good of all, socialist feminism offers a levelling up to all the oppressed and exploited in society.

CONCLUSIONS

Intersectionality means different things to different people. It has broadened in scope since its conception as a way to challenge the marginalisation of black women. Sometimes it is the partner of privilege theory, whereas amongst other feminists it is just one tool of analysis in a broader toolbox.

We shouldn't discard the "rational kernel within the mystical shell" and should be mindful of the context of intersectionality's popularity.

HELOISA HELENA (1962-)

Was involved in the student movement against the military dictatorship in Brazil, before joining the Workers' Party (PT). She became a leader of Socialist Democracy, a Trotskyist caucus inside the PT. Heloísa Helena was elected a federal senator in 1998 and became a leading critic of Lula's PT government after 2002. She and other critics were expelled from the PT in 2003, going on to found the Socialism and Freedom Party (PSOL) in 2004. Heloísa Helena was the president of PSOL from 2004 to 2010, and PSOL's candidate for president in the 2006 general elections. She stood as PSOL candidate for senator of Alagoas in 2014.

Despite the rise of dramatic social movements across the globe, labour organisations, aimed at fighting for the working class, remain a marginal force. Marxist arguments about the central role of the working class in forcing change remain obscure to many activists.

Intersectionality, though it has, as we have seen, been around for a long time, became popular in the context of the 2010 upsurge of student and workers' struggles both in the UK and internationally, with the inspirational Arab Spring. The layer of activists brought into struggle were then disappointed and disillusioned after 2011 as many international struggles took a reactionary turn and workers' fights in the UK were sold out by the trade union bureaucracy. It is not surprising that people look to more "winnable" and achievable changes such as improved individual inter-personal relationships.

Importantly, intersectionality also emerged in response to prejudice and ignorance in movements, and a failure of socialist organisations to tackle this (and at their worst reinforcing the oppression). Undoubtedly, the continued mishandling and minimising of sexism and violence against women in the left and labour movement, brought into sharper focus more recently, have played a role in turning young feminists "off" Marxism and "on" to intersectionality.

Intersectionality is not entirely wrong, but it is incomplete. It fails to push at the contradictions between particular experiences and identities and the universal and structural. Oppression isn't just created by individuals' locations but by the inter-relationships between people, and between people and the systems in society.

A focus on identity as the lens of struggle, combined with an alternative, identity-based concept of class, means that the possibility of abolishing, or even seriously fighting, the problem disappears. Struggle takes the form of equality among groups at best, or simply striving for changes in inter-personal relationships at worst. The fight for significant and transformative change is side-lined, along with the idea of how this could be possible — ideas, solidarity and struggle.

Socialist feminism and Marxism already hold the possibility of a full, "intersectional" analysis and movement. The ideas of intersectionality add little to socialist feminism, and the label now carries significant baggage. But thinking about intersectionality theory may be useful in reminding us that Marxism has not always lived up to its full potential and, through this, helping us to be clear about what kind of Marxism and movement we are fighting for.

FURTHER READING

bell hooks (1981) *Ain't I a Woman?: Black women and feminism*
Kimberlé Crenshaw, 'Mapping the Margins: intersectionality, identity politics and violence against women of colour' (bit.ly / crenshaw-margins)
Janine Booth, 'Festival of the oppressed', in Workers' Liberty's *We Stand for Workers' Liberty* (bit.ly / wl-festival)

IS "PATRIARCHY" USEFUL?

BY CARMEN BASANT

Aside from the specific details, the approach shown by Engels in *The Origin of the Family, Private Property and the State* (1984) is crucial for socialist feminism today. Engels' concern, and our concern, is that the position of women is shaped by ever-changing material conditions of existence.

In contrast, the radical feminist understanding of patriarchy, as a primary and predetermined structure that has existed in all societies throughout history, diverts us from the fact that women have agency and can transform their situation as a sex and gender.

Women's oppression was present in pre-capitalist societies, and historical work to trace the origins and nature of this oppression is important. But in capitalist societies, changed material conditions have generated distinct forms of oppression for women. Capitalism oppresses women in new ways — in the commodification of the body, for example. Capitalism has also produced conditions for women to enter the workplace, such that women have the opportunity to become economically independent and to discuss their social position with other women and to organise to change it.

In our early Workers' Liberty pamphlet, *The Case for Socialist Feminism*, we critique Heidi Hartmann's "dual systems" theory: that society is a dual system of capitalism and patriarchy. Referencing Iris Marion Young, who troubles over the separation of struggles against patriarchy and capitalism, we comment: "Even the most 'feminist' issues, like fighting for abortion rights and against sexual harassment at work, are inseparable from the general struggle for democracy and socialism."

With the work of Sheila Rowbotham, we summate our problem with patriarchy — defined as a fixed structure — as returning us (and indeed, reducing us) to biology. However, I do not think we fully resolve our position on patriarchy, or rather, we do not consider whether any conceptualisation of patriarchy might be of analytical use.

WIDER DEBATE ON CAPITALISM AND PATRIARCHY

Iris Marion Young argues ('Unruly Categories: A Critique of Nancy Fraser's Dual Systems Theory') that we should: "conceptualize issues of justice involving recognition and identity as having inevitably material economic sources and consequences, without thereby being reducible to market dynamics or economic exploitation and deprivation."

The feminist debate Young engages with aims to overcome the disjuncture between economic reductionism (that disregards "the cultural") and identity politics (which overlooks "the economic"). The debate explores how one frames political struggles for cultural recognition and economic redistribution. Young rejects a social-theoretical distinction between the cultural and the economic. Counter to this Nancy Fraser ('From Redistribution to Recognition? Dilemmas of

GRUNWICK AND JAYABEN DESAI

Grunwick was a film processing plant in North London, whose workers were mainly women and mainly Asian. They worked in terrible conditions for poverty wages under a whip-cracking bully manager without the protection of a union. In the long, hot summer of 1976, the workload and the factory became unbearable. A few workers walked out, others joined them.

Jayaben Desai, who was to become one of the leaders of the strike, was among them. Instead of just leaving she made a speech to the other workers and then went to their manager and said: "What you are running here is not a factory, it is a zoo. But in a zoo there are many types of animals. Some are monkeys who dance on your fingertips, others are lions who can bite your head off. We are the lions, Mr. Manager". And so began a two year-long strike for better conditions and union recognition.

Demonstrating mountainous courage, the women organised mass pickets and hunger strikes. They had solidarity from thousands of workers across the labour and feminist movements. But, undermined by police brutality, demonisation in the media, and an unreliable trade union leadership the Grunwick strikers lost.

But the labour movement as a whole gained:

• The strike knocked down many prejudices inside the movement against black and women workers.

• Grunwick put class struggle back on the agenda, after a lull.

• Grunwick raised questions of solidarity, the role of the state and police, and the importance of rank-and-file organisation in the trade unions which were key for the struggles that followed, and remain so today.

Justice in a "Post-Socialist" Age') sees "[s]truggles for recognition occur in a world of exacerbated material inequality", whilst stressing that we must figure out "how to conceptualize cultural recognition and social equality in forms that support rather than undermine one another". Accordingly, Fraser makes a helpful analytical distinction between demands for redistribution and recognition: "by distinguishing redistribution and recognition analytically, and by exposing their distinctive logics, I aim to clarify — and begin to resolve — some of the central political dilemmas of our age."

Bearing in mind Young's approach, the intersectionality turn within academic feminism broadens the definitions of capitalism and class to the economic and the cultural. As a result, there is no conceptual distinction between "race", ethnicity, sexuality, gender, and class, since all are seen as structures and ideologies of oppression. Yet class is not another ideology of oppression, it is fundamentally *a relation of exploitation*. And homophobia, racism, and sexism are all different kinds of oppression. For example, capitalism can accommodate a form of gay equality by accommodating significant numbers of gay people who deviate from the heteronormative norm of the nuclear family. The principal opponents to such gay equality today are not corporate but religious and cultural. On the other hand, capitalism could not tolerate the abolishment of social reproduction by domestic female labour.

There is some merit to Fraser's approach because she is able to spell out the historical specificity of capitalism:

"In precapitalist, pre-state societies, [...] status simply is the overarching principle of distribution and where the status order and the class hierarchy are therefore fused, misrecognition simply entails maldistribution. In capitalist societies, in contrast, where the institutionalization of specialized economic relations permits the relative uncoupling of economic distribution from structures of prestige, and where status and class can therefore diverge, misrecognition and maldistribution are not fully mutually convertible" ('Heterosexism, Misrecognition, and Capitalism: A Response to Judith Butler').

Moreover, Fraser is able to distinguish between different forms of oppression and exploitation in capitalist society. On class: "The task of the proletariat [...] is not simply to cut itself a better deal, but 'to abolish itself as a class'. The last thing it needs is recognition of its difference".

On sexuality: "Sexuality in this conception is a mode of social differentiation whose roots do not lie in the political economy, as homosexuals are distributed throughout the entire class structure of capitalist society, occupy no distinctive position in the division of labour, and do not constitute an exploited class. Rather, their mode of collectivity is that of a despised sexuality, rooted in the cultural-valuational structure of society. [...] the injustice they suffer is quintessentially a matter of recognition" ('From Redistribution...').

On "race": "How can anti-racist groups fight simultaneously to abolish 'race' and to valorize racialized group specificity?"

And, finally, on gender, Fraser ('How feminism has become capitalism's handmaiden') queries: "we might disrupt the passage from our critique of economism to identity politics by integrating the struggle to transform a status order premised on masculinist cultural values with the struggle for economic justice."

CONCLUSIONS

In *The Case for Socialist Feminism*, we made the following, still-pertinent point: "Women have been oppressed for thousands of years. Possibly they resisted the beginnings of oppression with violence. For sure individual women have always kicked back and stood up for themselves. But the programme of women's liberation dates from capitalist societies. […] Capitalism continued the oppression of women, but changed it."

Central to our programme for women's liberation is an understanding of the distinct conditions of existence created by capitalism. There is explanatory worth in integrating into our analysis of the social inequalities of gender, a concept of patriarchy — as structures of male status and power over women, often pre-capitalist and/or religious in origin — which have come to *both fuse and collide* with capitalist social relations and forces.

Empirical realities in recent years, such as the anti-abortion movement in the United States, the variation of violence against women across the world, and the phenomenon of organised sexual abuse networks run by groups of British Pakistani men, indicate such an intersection, fusion and collision of capitalism and patriarchy.

REFERENCES/FURTHER READING

Young, I. M. (1997) 'Unruly Categories: A Critique of Nancy Fraser's Dual Systems Theory' *New Left Review* 222

Fraser, N. (1995) 'From Redistribution to Recognition? Dilemmas of Justice in a "Post-Socialist" Age' *New Left Review* 212

Fraser, N. (1997) 'Heterosexism, Misrecognition, and Capitalism: A Response to Judith Butler' *Social Text* 15(3/4)

Fraser, N. (2013) 'How feminism has become capitalism's handmaiden'. *Guardian*, 14 October 2103. Available at: www.theguardian.com/commentisfree/2013/oct/14/feminism-capitalist-handmaiden-neoliberal

SEX-POSITIVE FEMINISM

BY RACHAEL CLARK

This is a summary of two strands of feminist thought that have tackled the subject of sexuality since the 1960s and 1970s. These two approaches — sex-positive feminism and radical feminism — have been in direct conflict with one another. The 1980s "sex wars" over attitudes to pornography were underpinned by that conflict.

Socialist feminist Lynne Segal, writing from the sex-positive point of view, described the distinction between radical and sex-positive feminism as resting on, "the place given to men and their sexuality as the root of women's oppression as against the rejection of any such single orientation".

Radical feminism analyses sexuality outside of social and historical context; it thinks, more-or-less, the fundamental inequality in society is men's oppression of women. Radical feminism believes that men's control is enacted through innate "male" qualities, such as aggressive sexuality. It blames women's oppression on male *behaviour* as well as power. This leads to radical feminism's focus on changing and controlling what men, and all of us, are allowed to do in society. It tells men, "Don't buy pornography" (and might try to ban it). It may condemn relationships and practices that, as they see it, reinforce the power men wield through sex, such as sex work, or even heterosexuality. This feminist condemnation spills over into condemning sex workers and heterosexual women themselves. It does not recognise that women have agency in these relationships and thus is immensely pessimistic about the ability of women to control our bodies and sexualities.

Sex-positive feminism, on the other hand, situates sexuality in a social and historical context; it believes society's structures play a role in shaping women's oppression. It also looks for opportunities for struggle — class struggle, mass women's movements, solidarity between women and between women and men — to challenge the oppressive framework that surrounds women's lives and sexualities.

By seeking to overthrow oppression through social struggle, sex-positive feminism places far less emphasis than radical feminism on controlling individual behaviour. This connects to sex-positive feminism's second key element: its liberalism and emphasis on women's empowerment. It argues against censorship of sexual material. It has human sympathy with women's sexual expressions, even those, such as rape fantasies, which seem to "buy in" to oppressive gender relations. It challenges the sexism of mass culture in general, not just those aspects that "sexualise" women. It understands that, while sexualised women's bodies abound in Western capitalist culture, social and religious conservatism continue to restrict sexuality in general, and women's sexuality in particular. In this context, it values the struggle that women wage to carve out a space in which to enjoy sex and control our bodies. This perspective emphasises women's agency and potential power to determine our individual sexualities and to transform the oppressive conditions that shape our lives.

For its dual emphasis on social transformation and women's empowerment, sex-positive feminism is a strand of feminist thought we in Workers' Liberty feel we can learn much from.

This summary traces pro-sex and radical feminist positions as they developed in response to each other and against their political backdrop, from the ideas of sexual liberation in second wave feminism through to the sex wars of the 1980s. It looks at writings which further developed sex-positive feminist ideas. It considers a more modern incarnation of radical feminism in criticisms of "objectification" and so-called "raunch culture". It concludes by exploring how we can apply a sex-positive approach, for women's greater social and sexual empowerment, to issues of sexuality and women's oppression today.

SECOND WAVE FEMINISM

Many second wave feminists were socialists, inspired by political and class struggle, such as the Ford sewing machinists' equal pay strike in 1968. Without calling themselves sex-positive feminists, writers and activists of the women's liberation movement articulated elements of a sex-positive perspective.

First, they fought for sexual liberation within the context of broader social struggle. They demanded — and in some cases won — birth control, abortion on demand, equal pay, and other measures for economic and social independence that resulted in greater sexual autonomy. Juliet Mitchell describes how they fought on "all fronts" against "all the major dimensions of women's oppression: economic, legal and sexual" (*Women's Estate*).

Second, they promoted women's sexual empowerment by integrating sexual experience into political struggle. They challenged the male bias of 1960s sexual liberation. Sheila Rowbotham recalls that the climate of 1968 prompted women's "rediscovery of ...our own sexuality". She says this perception "entered politics" for the first time. She recalls seeing "scrawled on a bog wall in a sit-in" the demand: "Give me back my past, my childhood, my body, my life" (*Promise of a Dream*). The movement enabled women to understand their collective experience of sexuality for the first time, which was an important building block for the element of sex-positive feminism that promotes women's sexual empowerment.

RADICAL FEMINISM

By the late 1970s, the women's liberation movement had fragmented, against the backdrop of rising right-wing neoliberalism and setbacks for the working class. Radical or revolutionary feminism, present throughout the 1970s, emerged as the dominant current; emphasis shifted from the "shared needs and struggles" of the second wave "towards an exploration of difference" (Jeffrey Weeks, *Sex, Politics and Society*). Lynne Segal, a writer who fought back against this new current in the 1980s, subsequently analysed this shift as a "reaction to more conservative times and the setbacks faced by feminist activism, especially in the US" (where anti-pornography feminism arose). (Lynne Segal, 'Only the Literal', in *More Dirty Looks*).

The new "radical" current asserted that the difference between women and men was primarily expressed and created through men's and women's different sexualities. It rejected the second wave's integration of sexuality into social structures. Instead, it built on the myth that women and men have timeless sexual natures. Male sexuality was seen as excessive and dangerous. Female sexuality was seen as passive and pure. Lynne Segal writes that radical feminism declared "women's original innocence" (*Is the Future Female?*). This echoed late 19th-century "feminist social purity", which labelled men's sexuality as uncontrollable and women's as a benign urge for motherhood, exemplified in the title of Christabel Pankhurst's pamphlet, *Votes for women, chastity for men!* (Jeffrey Weeks, *Sex, Politics and Society*).

Writers such as Catharine MacKinnon and Andrea Dworkin, who took the helm of this radical current, asserted that sexuality was the source of men's oppression of women: "sexuality is the set of practices that inscribes gender as unequal in social life". (Micaela di Leonardo and Roger Lancaster, *Socialist Feminist Reader: Gender, Sexuality, Political Economy*). In their narrative, male sexual acts, from penetration to rape, were the tool that produced the significant oppressive relationship, oppression of all women by all men. The 1979 pamphlet *Political Lesbianism: The Case Against Heterosexuality* argued that oppression was so inherent in sexuality that "giving up fucking" was a feminist's only method of "taking your politics seriously". Heterosexuality is inevitably an exercise of men's power, Dworkin insisted: for women, "getting fucked and being owned are inseparably the same" (Mandy Merck, 'From Minneapolis to Westminster').

ANTI-PORNOGRAPHY AGITATION

From such a position, it was logical that radical feminists should gravitate towards a focus on pornography in the 1980s. Porn was seen to symbolise and elevate the exercise of male sexuality. Dworkin argued that, in pornography, "the woman's sex is appropriated, her body is possessed" and "the penis is a symbol of terror". (*Is the Future Female?*). With mixed success, MacKinnon and Dworkin proposed Ordinances in several US federal legislatures to give women who felt pornography's harm the power to sue its makers. The Minneapolis Ordinance, proposed in 1983, assailed pornography for depicting "the sexually explicit subordination of women". It went on to say:

"...pornography is central in creating and maintaining the civil inequality of the sexes. Pornography is a systematic practice of exploitation and subordination based on sex, which differentially harms women......in employment, education etc." (Mandy Merck, 'From Minneapolis to Westminster').

Pornography was held responsible for violence against women and women's oppression more generally. MacKinnon held this up as "a new theory of social causality" (Mandy Merck 'From Minneapolis to Westminster').

"THE SEX WARS"

Drawing on second wave feminism's instinct to liberate sexuality, "sex-positive feminism" took shape throughout the 1980s. In debates so fierce that they acquired the label "the sex wars", sex-positive feminists challenged the anti-pornography position on a number of issues.

They challenged the disproportionate emphasis placed on sexual, compared to non-sexual, depictions of sexism in mass culture, arguing that the sexual focus was "reactionary" and "simply reproduced" the "assumptions and ideology in dominant culture" (Elizabeth Wilson in *Sex Exposed...*). They challenged anti-pornography feminists' emphasis on representations, rather than lived oppressions. They rejected what they saw as "pessimism" in the conclusion that men's power is innate, unconquerable and inevitably expressed through sex. They resisted illiberal attempts to restrict the circulation of pornographic material, which would, as Segal said, grant "powers of the moral right to police 'deviant' sexualities" (*Is the Future Female?*).

In a recent article, Lynne Segal reflects that the "sex wars" were a "deadlocked debate", which was "at bedrock about competing feminist foundations: the place given to men and their sexuality as the root of women's oppression, as against the rejection of any such single orientation"('Only the Literal: The Contradictions of Anti-pornography Feminism').

SEX-POSITIVE FEMINISM

In the 1980s some writers transcended the limits of this deadlocked debate. From challenging the idea that oppression stems from a simplistic, sexual cause, Lynne Segal, Jeffrey Weeks, Gayle Rubin and others went on to develop a nuanced sex-positive perspective, sympathetic to the social and human complexity surrounding sexuality and optimistic about our ability to transform sexuality on an individual and social level.

They explored sexuality in its complexity. Not only did they dispute that all heterosexual sex is inherently oppressive, they also refuted the idea that rape or domination fantasies were an acceptance of women's domination in real life. Lynne Segal insisted that the "connection between symbol and fantasy, experience and behaviour [is] complex": "neither women's nor men's sexual fantasies reflect simply the reality of male dominance and misogyny" (*Is the Future Female?*). Segal argued that we can have an element of autonomy over our sexual desires. This accepts women's choices without judgement, permitting "resistance, subversion and pleasure" (*Socialist Feminist Reader*), which were precluded by radical feminism. This articulates a key element of sex-positive feminism: emphasis on women's empowerment over sexual action and expression.

These writers also argued that sexuality does not cause oppression, but is itself oppressed. In *Thinking Sex: Notes for a Radical Theory of the Politics of Sexuality*, Gayle Rubin argues that, in Western societies, sexual oppression is shaped through systems of "sexual stratification" which "delimit a very small portion of human sexual capacity as sanctifiable". Oppression flows from "sexual standards". Religion enforces the standard of "procreative marriage"; mainstream psychology enforces "mature heterosexuality". She says radical feminism's standard that everyone should be a lesbian is just as objectionable as compulsory heterosexuality. She wants to work towards an acceptance of "sexual variety". This builds on her 1975 essay, *Traffic in Women*, which challenged the "system of compulsory heterosexuality" as "a system of oppression... as enduring as its nearest relative, sexism" (*Socialist Feminist Reader*). Rubin challenges Western culture's disproportionate focus on sex as a negative, destructive force, a definer of morality, a source of stigma for those at the bottom of the "sexual hierarchy", such as LGBTQ people and sex workers.

From Rubin's perspective, sex is not a mystical marker of our morality, separate from our identity. It is part of our material, human life, which we can understand and therefore control to some degree. More broadly, an understanding of how social forces produce sexual oppression enables collective struggle for sexual freedom. This element of sex-positive feminism integrates individual, social and sexual empowerment.

These writers situated sexuality in social and historical contexts. Jeffrey Weeks' *Sex, Politics and Society*, first published in 1981, is an account of the shaping of sexual lives by society since the late 18th century. In the preface to the 2012 edition, he recalls that when initially writing the book, "One of my prime aims…was to treat sexuality not as something esoteric and set apart… but as firmly located in wider social life".

Weeks describes how 19th-century society defined women's sexuality through "ideological articulation, medical and legal practices and moral endeavour", which "intersected at that crucial site for Victorian ideology, the family". To avoid "fraudulent claims upon property", women's "chastity" was enforced. He explains that, "female sexuality was necessarily therefore defined within… social and economic considerations". Weeks' illustration that women were made socially vulnerable through chastity standards shows us how definitions of acceptable female sexuality contributed to women's inequality. In contrast to radical feminist assertions that men's sexuality is a timeless oppressor, Weeks' analysis seeks to explain why sexuality is so often a site of men's power over women. Whereas radical feminists restrict the route to women's liberation to "simply focusing on sexual acts", this analysis seeks to understand and therefore "change the context of sexual relationships" (*Is the Future Female?*, quoting Weeks). Weeks provides an illustration of the aspect of sex-positive feminism that conceives of the struggle for greater sexual freedom within a struggle to overhaul the social institutions that oppress sexuality.

ANTI-OBJECTIFICATION FEMINISM

In his updated edition of *Sex, Politics and Society*, when Weeks notes that "a new culture of sexual pleasure, explicitness and conspicuous consumption" had become "increasingly normalised" since he wrote his first edition in 1981. He observes the expansion of online pornography and an increasingly sexualised popular culture.

Responding to this climate, much of the mainstream feminist movement has focused on sexual objectification. This term, while lacking clear definition, is seen by campaigners in an almost universally negative sense. It is commonly defined in terms of the passivity of the "object" (the woman) and the active agency of the "subject" (the male). In one definition, it treats women "as a body (or collection of body parts) valued predominantly for its use (or consumption) by others" (Fredrickson and Roberts, *Objectification theory: Toward understanding women's lived experiences and mental health risks*). It defines the objectifying gaze as played out through human interactions, representations of human relationships in the media and, most "perniciously", through "visual media that spotlight women's bodies and body parts and seamlessly align viewers with an implicit sexualizing gaze" (Fredrickson and Roberts, *Objectification theory…*).

Anti-objectification campaigners have focused on the sexualised images of women in "lads' mags", such as *Nuts* and *Zoo*. In the early 2000s, a number of university women's campaigns tried to move the mags to newsagents' top shelves. UK Feminista and Object launched "Lose the Lads' Mags", which pressured the Co-operative to cease stocking *Front* and *Nuts*, causing both magazines to lose sales and fold by 2014. In 2015, the *No More Page 3* petition has more than 200,000 signatures.

Challenging the sexist attitudes peddled by these publications is an undeniably feminist cause; it echoes the way our sisters from the second wave took direct action to remove sexist pin-ups from walls in their workplaces. However, the strand of feminism that targets "objectification" and identifies a related enemy in so-called "raunch culture" borrows much of its rationale from anti-pornography feminism. These campaigns and writings pull towards politically limited aims and conservative conclusions. In two ways, they incline in the opposite direction from the social transformation and sexual empowerment pursued by sex-positive feminism.

When *Nuts* folded, Sophie Bennett, Acting Director of UK Feminista, commented: "sexist, pornographic lads' mags promote attitudes underpinning violence against women. They normalise the deeply harmful idea that it's acceptable to treat women as a sum of body parts". She attributes causality to imagery, an echo of the anti-pornography assertion that porn causes violence against women. This logic omits the oppressive social structures that produce women's inequality. Anti-objectification campaigns therefore restrict their aims to removing objectifying images. To leave oppressive structures unchallenged, but merely aim to obliterate specifically sexualised representations of women, is politically limited and reinforces already-dominant, conservative attitudes about women's sexuality. This is the first way in which anti-objectification campaigns' conservative conclusions diverge from the social and sexual transformation sought by sex-positive feminism.

Ariel Levy's influential *Female Chauvinist Pigs: Women and the Rise of Raunch Culture* exemplifies the second way in which anti-objectification logic inverts the progressive potential offered by sex-positive feminism. Levy's prime target is women's sexualised behaviour; in targetting this, she attacks the very notion of women's sexual empowerment promoted by sex-positive feminism. She directs her ire towards Female Chauvinist Pigs (FCPs), "women who make sex objects of other women and ourselves", who are overtly sexual in the "tawdry, tarty, cartoonlike" manner promoted by an increasingly sexualised popular culture, "raunch culture". Levy is incensed that women's claims for empowerment through sexualised culture are in some ways tolerated. She mocks, "And good news! — being part of it (i.e. raunch culture) makes you a strong, powerful woman. Because we have determined that all empowered women must be overtly and publicly sexual".

Rather than acknowledging women's agency as a positive, Levy complains that to be "hot", women don't just have to "*yield* approval", but "actively seek" it and give off the vibe that "any attention you receive for your physicality is welcome". Levy chooses to target the limited sense of control that women who want sexual attention are obtaining. In the name of feminism, Levy would shut down the limited taste of empowerment that women claim from being willingly, publicly sexual.

Women in Workers' Liberty do not think that "raunch culture" is a vehicle to women's liberation; it bears the hallmarks of the sexism of wider society. However, we are sympathetic to women who, grappling for a sense of sexual empowerment, reach for the sexual modes easiest to hand, those supplied and infected by the sexism of the dominant culture. We want to overturn sexist society, but, until such time as we do, we defend women's right to be sexual — even if sexualisation takes sexist forms — in defiance of still-dominant conservative prescriptions to cover up. Levy assails our sex-positive perspective with her disdain for the limited degree of empowerment that women are grasping from within a sexist context.

WOMEN'S SITUATION TODAY

Women today struggle to be sexual in a contradictory climate. On the one hand, as Weeks notes, in recent decades, social conservatism surrounding issues such as extra-marital sex has eroded; "sexuality ....is more open to diversity, choice and creativity". However, women have not won sufficient social equality to remove the sexism and stigma attached to female sexuality. Weeks observes that there is a contradiction between the greater circulation of sexual — mostly sexist — images of women, and women's social position.

Women are left to negotiate a sense of sexual identity in a sexualised — yet sexist and conservative — culture:

"Despite the undoubted trend towards greater sexualisation of female bodies, women, especially working class women, still... struggle against persistent gendered notions of respectability and sexual decency". (Bev Skeggs, *Formations of Class and Gender: Becoming Respectable*).

Assertive "female pop groups" celebration of "autonomy, sexual desire and female pleasure" has not translated to the experience of "young people's lives" (Weeks). The real root of most — primarily working-class — women's lack of sexual agency is that we still lack power in our lives. Our sex-positive perspective sees that women struggle for sexual autonomy within a sexist framework, within a context where we do not have much control over any aspect of life. Our perspective sees women's attempts at autonomy as a kernel of potential, which we wish to highlight and cultivate.

This kernel of sexual empowerment has found expression in several recent movements.

In January 2011, a police officer advised students at Toronto's York University to "avoid dressing like sluts in order not to be victimised". Sick of victim-blaming, a group of young women organised a protest of 4,000 people — "Slutwalk". It sparked protests world-wide in countries such as the USA, Brazil and the UK.

The protesters were overwhelmingly young women, angry that sexual assault is trivialised; that women are not respected; that they are pressured to be stereotypically "sexy" then get branded as "sluts". Controversially, some women on the protests dressed as "sluts" trying to subvert the slur. Women in Workers' Liberty welcomed and joined the SlutWalks. It was empowering to demand to dress as we choose — to look sexy if we choose — without shame or fear.

Along similar lines, in 2014, schools that labelled women's "anatomy" as a "distraction" from the "learning environment" provoked protest by introducing dress codes banning short skirts, tight trousers and revealing tops. Girls at South

Orange Middle School in New Jersey started the campaign, "I am more than a distraction". Another group of students defied a ban on tight trousers, carrying posters through their school that asked, "Are my pants lowering your test scores?"

There has been a growing awareness of the issue of street harassment. In a 2013 UN survey, 99.3% of Egyptian women reported being subject to sexual harassment. In India, a survey conducted after the gang rape in Delhi in 2012 showed that 70% of Indian women had been sexually harassed. The protests following the Delhi rape case have sparked a growing women's movement in India. In New York, the campaign "Stop Street Harassment" is giving voice to women who say: *I will walk down the street and be sexy if I want, but do not sexualise me against my will.*

These campaigns demonstrate that there are a number of social forces at play: young, working-class women's lack of social power; the sexist attitudes of schools, police and authorities; the designation of women to the "private" realm so we're socialised to feel uncomfortable in public. All these social forces converge on our bodies so that our sexuality feels like it is being used against us. Yet, simultaneously, women find a glimmer of bodily autonomy. As a collective, women are able to assert their right to wear what they want without being sexualised; to be "sexy" without being judged. It is this element of empowerment that sex-positive feminism seeks to emphasise. The example of India shows us how the struggle to transform sexual relations can be integrated into broader social transformation for women.

CONCLUSION

A sex-positive approach that promotes women's sexual empowerment and analyses sexuality within a social framework is a far more powerful tool for our liberation, than an approach which has a sex-shaming logic at its core. That can only rob most women of the precious, albeit limited, sense of sexual agency we can attain in the sexist society that surrounds us.

We've seen that feminists of the second wave took the greatest strides towards sexual freedom because they had a women's and workers' movement in which to struggle for social and economic independence. It is no coincidence that as these movements declined, radical and anti-pornography feminists abandoned the terrain of social struggle and limited themselves to maligning sex. Unfortunately, from the 1980s onwards, sex-positive feminists have lacked a movement with enough social power to challenge the oppressive framework that surrounds sexuality. Hence, versions of radical feminism, with their emphasis on sexuality and objectification, have persisted. We in Workers' Liberty seek to renew and expand the women's movement.

In the immediate term we can continue to critique the conservative implications of campaigns that focus on sexual images and behaviour in isolation from a social framework. We can develop our sex-positive approach, analysing sexual oppression in relation to social structures and applying this to the situations and movements in which women are struggling today.

WOMEN WORKERS OF THE WORLD, UNITE!

BY JOAN TREVOR

Women workers are vital to the success of globalised capitalism — they make a huge portion of its profits! Even after the global recession that followed the 2008 crash, women's participation in the world's workforce continues to increase. Capitalist enterprises, big and small, are using the cheap and flexible nature of women's waged labour.

The ways that capitalism today, in its globalised neoliberal phase, exploits women are not the same as in earlier epochs of capitalist expansion. Indeed capitalism has managed to make the conditions of vast numbers of all workers more precarious, and driven down wages across the working class. While the forms of waged work have massively expanded — no longer confined to a small range of manual jobs in highly specific industries or domestic work — global labour markets are still highly gender segregated. Migrant and BME workers are also in "feminised" areas of the job market: cleaning, burger flipping and care work.

While women graduates may find jobs in management, those jobs are more in Human Resources management; in bio-sciences rather than computer sciences.

Women workers are still a vast army of cheap waged workers and they make up the majority of workers in the unregulated informal economy — petty trading, sex work, cash-in-hand service work.

Behind gender segregation, as we argue elsewhere, are the historical and present realities of women's unpaid labour in the household. Globalisation reinscribes our low paid and flexible status as women workers. And in a world where very few places have subsidised or free, good quality childcare and where social safety nets have been slashed, women are getting poorer, their lives more insecure and burdensome.

Capitalism throughout the world, even within the same country, exists in the full range of its stages, with, at the pinnacle, the vast, highly advanced technological factories producing goods such as iPads and mobile phones, existing just up the road from mean workshops where workers are likely to endure the worst conditions. In between the two we find hangars filled with sewing machines where mainly women workers make clothes for sale in richer countries, often working for subcontractors fulfilling contracts for high street brand names. Capitalism still needs this range, as, in order to function, the bigger assembly plants require the components made in the smaller workshops. At the same time, in the "globalised workplace" conditions in all parts of the chain are driven down, from the components factory in Bangladesh to the shopfloor in Oxford Street where goods are sold.

The variety is immense but the workers in all of these different settings, men, women and — though it is illegal almost everywhere — even children have common interests: to get better pay, better conditions, more control over their workplace, health and safety measures, and ultimately, control over the whole of society, through political action — for democracy and for more, for socialism!

This diversity in workers' conditions, in the way they live their lives, can bewilder, and make it hard for workers around the world to relate to each other as people with a common interest. The diversity of experiences is reflected more and more in the phenomenon of mass labour migration.

In earlier epochs this would happen between regions of one country; now it occurs between regions of the world with very different levels of wealth.

It is a major part of the job of socialists to point out what all workers have in common, to foster solidarity between workers, wherever in the world they live. It is also part of our task to foster solidarity between men and women workers.

Since the early days capitalists have often favoured women workers and children in factories for their nimble fingers but also because capitalism made use of pre-existing inequality: for example, the capitalists believed women workers would be easier to boss around than men and less inclined to join unions; and capitalists have used sexual harassment by mainly male overseers to police women's work, particularly at times when jobs were hard to come by.

Being a waged worker could be a liberating experience, not because it freed women from domestic responsibilities but because it brought women into the potentially more social world of the factory and workplace. But it was not very liberating unless women and men fought alongside each other, both concerned to alter the conditions of work for all. More usually, even with new relative freedoms — and sometimes because of them — women had to work hard to make the labour movement fight in battles with them.

The model of capitalist change is different now but class struggle is alive. The ruling capitalists have learned lessons to apply in today's epoch of globalised capitalism, to keep one step ahead of the workers — and so must we learn the lessons the history of the workers' movement teaches us. We need to examine how the ideas and forms of organisation we have developed can apply to today's women workers in globalised capitalism — how to assimilate, adapt and make them real in today's globalised capitalist world — and how to make the most of new forms of struggle.

We hope to do this in a way that can help us to build solidarity between workers — women workers, in particular — the world round.

Women workers brought into the ambit of capitalism are becoming more politically active. They are helping to build new parties and influence existing ones.

TASLIMA NASRIN (1962-)

Taslima Nasrin is a Bangladeshi feminist and critic of political Islamism. A former gynaecologist, in 1993 she published the novel Lajja (Shame), describing a Hindu family persecuted by Muslims. She was driven out of Bangladesh by death threats from Islamists and exiled in Sweden and Germany. She lived in Kolkata, West Bengal in India between 2004 and 2007 but was targeted by Islamist demonstrators and put under house arrest by government authorities. After Al-Queda issued death threats against her, Nasrin moved to the USA.

Small socialist currents exist in developing countries such as Indonesia and Kurdistan. Socialists in developed countries should do everything that we can to support such currents. This doesn't just mean paying lip service to their struggles; it means raising money for them, it means defending them against their bosses in industrial struggles, against their states when they are repressed, and against formations such as Islamic State in the Middle East and Boko Haram in Nigeria that threaten their very existence.

We must push our trade unions to support the struggles of workers in every country.

Workers' political organisations in developing countries are often in their early stages and they face huge challenges but with adequate class politics and answers to the political questions posed to workers, even small organisations can wield great power in a short time. The history of the Russian Social-Democratic Labour Party (the revolutionary socialists, the Bolsheviks) shows it. It took decades of women's and socialist struggle to achieve things such as the eight-hour working day or universal suffrage in the developed capitalist countries. It need not take women workers in the new globalised capitalism so long if they can stand on the shoulders of the giants who have gone before!

Convinced socialists, such Workers' Liberty, must debate with the new workers' movements, share our understanding of the experiences, the successes and failures of previous socialist movements, and learn from the new workers' movements, so that together we can build a force that can put an end to globalised capitalism.

GLOBALISATION

"Globalisation" is a multi-faceted integration of capitalism affecting almost every country. The start date of "globalisation" is debated but, certainly, since the late 1970s capitalism has expanded anew, spread throughout the world, to almost every country.

These are the basic features of globalisation:

• More integrated global markets, and more people working under capitalist social relations than ever before in history.

• The weight of multinational corporations (MNCs) — that plan their production and distribution on a global scale — is growing.

• Special Economic Zones have been set up in many countries — tax- and regulation-light regions in developing countries which house vast factories producing clothes, electronic goods, etc., for large foreign companies. MNCs "outsource" production from the countries where they are based to countries where the labour is cheaper.

• Supranational institutions such as the International Monetary Fund (IMF), the World Bank and World Trade Organisation (WTO), and regional trade blocs such as the European Union (EU) and North American Free Trade Agreement (NAFTA) play an increasing role in the development of the global economy.

• Neo-liberal government policies, such as austerity, privatisation and free trade, are applied almost universally.

As capitalism spreads across the globe, the working class becomes more numerous and more connected across borders by international production chains.

As during its earlier period of growth, capitalism today transforms the new areas of the world it dominates. Capitalism:

- changes the class structure of society, creating the industrial working class;
- causes huge movements of people from rural to urban areas, and international labour migration, including women;
- draws in more and more natural resources, and threatens the environment;
- transforms the lives of working people, women, especially.

Often, these changes, measured from the standpoint of the individual worker, are bad: "...the world is [not] being 'levelled up' to a uniform prosperity. Far from it. The ripping off of the workers and peasants of the ex-colonial countries continues, but with the Armani-suited international banker replacing the colonial soldier and tax collector. Today's 'imperialism of free trade' is the domination of rich over poor and richer nations over poorer nations, achieved primarily (to use a phrase from Marx) by 'the dull compulsion of economic relations. Direct force, outside economic conditions, is still used, but only in exceptional circumstances' — rather than as the rule, as it was under the 'high imperialism' of the late 19th century and the first half of the 20th century." (Workers' Liberty, *We Stand for Workers' Liberty*)

But, collectively, the working class is gaining in potential to reform its lives in the here and now, and to transform its collective conditions for good. Moreover, the wealth unleashed by capitalist production, wealth that workers can lay hold of and turn to good, is vast.

As a result of its position in the global production chain, the working class has tremendous power. It can bring capitalist production to a halt through strikes. In building labour movements, workers have shown the collective, democratic skills necessary to run society on the basis of need, not profit.

Capitalism forces workers to band together to defend their interests. Workers use strikes, sit-ins, factory occupations and demonstrations to challenge the rule of capital.

WORKERS' POWER, WORKERS' SOLIDARITY

The factory collapse in Rana Plaza, in the Bangladeshi capital Dhaka, on 24 April 2013, in which at least 1,138 Bangladeshi garment workers died, spurred people around the world to fight for better conditions for the world's 75 million garment workers.

Campaigning initiatives among the consumers of fashion in developed countries, such as Fashion Revolution Day, played a role in helping to achieve the Accord on Fire and Building Safety in Bangladesh, which makes independent safety inspections of 2,000 factories compulsory.

But the most powerful people forcing change have been Bangladeshi garment workers themselves, as they mounted a wave of protests and strikes in the wake of the Rana Plaza tragedy. The IndustriALL Global Union began a new trade union organising drive in Bangladesh with the slogan: "The stronger the union, the safer the factory!"

"Consumer power" existed in the early days of industrial capitalism as well. Middle-class and even aristocratic pressure in the 19th century played a role in forcing factory owners to treat workers better, but the key force in improving workers' lives, then as now, was workers themselves.

In her history of the 1888 Bryant & May match workers' strike, *Striking a Light*, Louise Raw explained how Annie Besant, a middle-class, Fabian socialist, was credited with the victory of the match workers when they went on strike, whereas in fact the match workers were already a self-organised workforce with a history of struggle, capable of winning by themselves.

After the strike, the match workers went on to found the Matchmakers' Union, and their dispute was one of the inspirations for the wave of "New Unionism" in the East End of London that culminated in the Great Dock Strike of 1889.

Action by the Bangladeshi garment workers in the wake of the Rana Plaza disaster has forced the Bangladesh government to legislate a higher minimum wage, and has been crucial in getting the Accord on Fire and Building Safety.

So what role can "solidarity" play, and what sort of solidarity do we need? We don't believe that British workers are different in significant ways from say, Bangladeshi or Chinese workers. A lot of campaigns concerned about the conditions that workers in developing countries work under don't recognise this. They talk about "consumer power", and think that the only way people in the UK can help those workers to have a better life is by spending our money "ethically", switching between brands, boycotting one or other, or buying so-called "fair trade" goods.

In reality, under capitalist methods of production, no brand is "ethical"; they are only more or less exploitative. Big corporations' Corporate Social Responsibility (CSR) statements and departments are more concerned with making the company look good than with helping workers — of course! The entire reason these companies exist is to exploit workers as much as possible so as to make the maximum profit.

We believe that the best way for workers to improve their living and working conditions, and raise their wages, is through organising in unions. That is true for workers in the UK and in countries such as Bangladesh and China. When those workers fight to organise, we support them!

We don't advocate boycotts of a particular country's products in the name of protecting our own country's products, even if — because of workers' past organisation — production is more "ethical" here.

We advocate levelling up to the best standards for workers globally. We want workers in developing countries to win what workers in developed countries won in the first 200 years of capitalism. And to go beyond, to work to transform the world and end exploitation altogether!

FARZANA BARI

Is vice president of the Awami Workers Party in Pakistan. The Awami Workers Party is a socialist political party formed in November 2012 through the merger of the Labour Party Pakistan, the Awami Party Pakistan and the Workers Party Pakistan. Bari is a well-known academic, writer and women's rights activist. The Awami Workers Party held its first women's convention in March 2014 to unveil the party's policy on the emancipation of women in Pakistan. Bari was elected vice president of the party at its first convention in September 2014.

GLOBAL WORKING-CLASS WOMEN'S MOVEMENT

We aim at a working-class women's movement — it will be a huge, international women's movement that encompasses workers in Europe, the US, and, increasingly, women workers in the vast globalised industries in the new factories in the "developing" countries, such as Bangladesh and China. The experience of these new women workers repeats a path followed in the first period of industrialisation in countries such as the UK, over the last 250 years — women workers, displaced from the countryside, move into the growing cities and find work in the new mills and factories of capitalist industrialisation.

These women are already following the path of struggle of earlier workers, organising strikes and protests and fledgling trade unions. We have a duty to

WORK SEGREGATION AND PAY INEQUALITY

The biggest shift in women's lives during the past 50 years has been in our participation in the labour market.

More women work than ever. In 1971, 53% of working-age women were in paid work, compared to over 67% in 2013. The corresponding figures for men are 92% and 76%. There is still a gender pay gap, of about 15% for full-time wages, more for part-time. After many years of decline, since 2010 the pay gap has been growing again. Some of the long-term decline in the pay gap is a product of falling wages for lower-paid men, as well as increasing numbers of women doing higher-paid work.

Although there has been some increase in the proportion of domestic work done by men, women still do more than two-thirds of housework. By and large, women's participation in the workforce has not led to a more equitable sharing of reproductive labour. It has rested instead on the exploitation of other women. Tasks such as childcare, caring for elderly relatives and cleaning are often contracted out to either unpaid female relatives, or waged workers (82% of workers in "caring, leisure and other services" are women).

Just as capital has encroached on the welfare state in the past few decades, so it has encroached on the territory of reproductive labour, turning roles that were once the province of the "housewife" into opportunities to make profit.

The overall figures on gender and pay mask significant class differences. Having children has far less impact on graduate women's pay than on the pay of lower-qualified women. Figures from a 2009 Equality and Human Rights Commission report suggest that a graduate woman with two children can expect to be paid 4% less than her child-free female equivalent, whereas for women with no qualifications and two children the impact on pay is 58%. (The idea that the disincentive applies to women is of course problematic, but given that statistically a woman is likely to be the lower-paid partner this is the reality for many heterosexual couples.)

In short, there are deep inequalities between women, as well as between women and men. Recognising these inequalities, assessing how they function and how to fight them, is essential to any serious project for women's liberation.

support and encourage that struggle but also, crucially, to learn from it. The militant struggles of Bangladeshi and Chinese workers today can be an inspiring contrast to the bureaucratised and beaten down labour movements in developed countries.

When we build solidarity for such workers, through raising money, publicising their struggles, and so on, we don't do it as an act of charity.

We have much to gain from their inspiring example, and we want to emphasise the common experiences of workers in newly industrialised countries and those of workers in countries such as the UK. Over centuries UK workers have climbed up from abject poverty, murderous exploitation, and crushing repression by their own efforts, and built political parties and trade unions to defend and represent their interests. The conditions and struggles of Bangladeshi and Chinese workers show us a mirror of our own past, how we toiled and how we fought. But if we do not struggle again and anew they could also show us our future: globalising capitalism bears in it the seeds of a race to the bottom — if, that is, workers in different countries and different parts of the world cannot develop solidarity with each other.

And as much as campaigns of solidarity with workers organising in the globalised industries are important means of support they are also, more crucially, ways that ideas and inspiration can spread.

Of course, much has changed since the early days of capitalist development. Women workers in globalising capitalism have the shoulders of giants to stand on — learning from earlier socialist and feminist pioneers.

Sometimes they appear to have the rulers of the world on their side! This appearance, however, is for the most part illusory.

The idea that all people should have equal rights regardless of gender is — almost — universal today; almost all countries enshrine it in their constitutions. The reality is often different: vast inequalities persist, what is on paper is often not practised. And socialists want to go beyond formal equality under capitalism, to true liberation, for humanity to fulfil its potential. Only socialism can achieve this.

International bodies such as the United Nations (UN) and the International Labour Organisation (ILO) represent the highest democratic ideals of the bourgeoisie at a global level. They fall far short of what socialists want and of what socialism could deliver. For example, they lay overwhelming emphasis on the importance of free trade and privatisation of nationalised industries and services as the way to improve the lot of all humanity. Whereas these policies in practice produce the opposite: inequality and immense suffering.

Socialists have fought to make the rights espoused in the politically progressive revolutionary phase of bourgeois history a reality for the majority, not just a

LIU JINGZHEN (1902-1979)

Joined the Chinese Communist Party and took part in the 1925-27 Revolution. She became a Trotskyist and helped organise the underground Chinese Trotskyist organisation in the 1930s and 1940s. Liu Jingzhen was arrested in 1952 by the Maoist government and imprisoned for five years. She joined her partner Zheng Chaolin in a labour camp during the 1960s. She was finally released in June 1979 and died six months later.

minority, and to go beyond fighting for political rights — for formal equality — to fighting for full economic and social equality.

Progress toward the fine-sounding goals laid out at international ruling-class conferences is agonisingly slow — of course it is, even the people who sign the fine documents do not believe that they will ever be held to account for not meeting those goals, or believe in granting real equality.

In the post-colonial era the new ruling classes in many of the countries that won their independence have pursued authoritarian, undemocratic drives to "modernise".

Often the impetus to this and the terms in which it has been discussed — by elites — is about what is good for the nation, development goals; sometimes the "national" interest is for women to be pressured into having more children if the population is considered to be too small or, conversely, to have fewer children where a country's rulers fear that population is too high and threatens development goals. In China, a "one child policy" existed from 1979 until very recently by which families were penalised if they have more than one child. (It was, first, relaxed and now is to be replaced by... a two-child policy!)

The One Child Policy was essentially state regulation of women's bodies, controlling population in order to minimise economic and other resources needed in the society.

Yet China hosted one of the major international conferences on women's rights, the 4th World Conference on Women, in Beijing in 1995. The irony that the state implementing the one-child policy hosted this major event is stark.

Nevertheless it is good that there are few countries where inequality between the sexes is openly espoused. And the widespread formal public commitment to equality of women — along with the widespread prejudice in favour of bourgeois democracy — one person, one vote — creates a better position from which to fight for women's rights. However, this is a foundation on which to build, and no cause for complacency.

Our struggle is to show that capitalism cannot deliver on its best ideals for the vast majority of the world's population. Indeed, it depends on exploiting workers for its continued existence. That is why we say we need a global working-class women's movement and seek to help build one!

FURTHER READING

www.tuc.org.uk/international-issues/labour-standards/international-trade-union-organisations/ethical-trade-and-fair

APPLE: WORKERS HAVE THE POWER

In recent years, multinational corporations (MNCs) have responded to the loud and just criticisms about the way they exploit and maltreat workers in globalised capitalism by setting up Corporate Social Responsibility (CSR) units. These are little more than Public Relations exercises to make the companies look good.

At the same time the highest organisations of world governance, bodies such as the United Nations (UN), even the International Labour Organisation (ILO), collaborate with big business in miseducating people about the role of capitalism and the place of workers' struggle in it.

Look on the ILO's website where they explain:

"The unique tripartite structure of the ILO gives an equal voice to workers, employers and governments to ensure that the views of the social partners are closely reflected in labour standards and in shaping policies and programmes."

An equal voice!

The chances of getting MNCs to respect workers or stop exploiting them is as likely as the lion lying down with the lamb. The only thing that brings bosses to the table to negotiate is workers organising and fighting them!

Yet, if you look at most of the publications of the ILO, you will find class struggle is invisible. Instead they talk about workers, and their exploiters and oppressors being partners!

When organisations do espouse women's and workers' rights, they make the case for them in terms of the advantages to business of integrating women: at the level of the factory, drawing them into the workforce, or promoting a few women to the highest echelons of a company.

It is true that going to work for wages can be empowering for women, but their independence and freedom are stifled again by the sheer hard work that they will have to do to earn a wage; the conditions under which they labour; the fact that their accommodation can be provided and policed by their bosses; and so on.

Going to work in a factory under globalisation will only be liberating to the degree that women fight to organise and push back against the bosses' motive of exploiting them to the maximum that s/he can in order to turn maximum profits.

As part of globalisation, companies such as Apple, through sub-contractors, exploit cheap labour in poorer countries to make their goods. Women workers make up a large number of those employed, and in the garment industry they are the overwhelming majority.

Adverse publicity, exposing abuses of workers, has pushed brands to worry about how they look but it is workers organising on the ground that really puts pressure on the brands to change their labour practices. A case study using Apple demonstrates this point.

Apple make large amounts of their goods in China, where workers have poor conditions at work and few rights to organise trade unions or democratic bodies. Apple first began producing an annual CSR report in 2007. In a four-page document they outlined their CSR targets and gave figures showing whether these targets were met (compliance). Year-on-year, the CSR reports got glossier and longer but, until 2012, the figures for non-compliance with their targets were shocking. The worst statistics showed routine flouting of Apple's maximum

	Target for maximum working hours per week per worker	Compliance (%)	Non-compliance (%)	Number of facilities audited	Number of pages in report
2007*	60	62	38	-	4
2008	60	32	68	39	14
2009	60	58	42	83	16
2010	60	46	54	102	24
2011	60	32	68	127	25
2012	60	38	62	229	27
2013	60	92	8	393	37
2014	60	95	5	451	40
2015	60	92	8	633	42

Facilities employing worked employed by Apple; subsequent years include directly employed and indirectly employed — i.e., workers working for sub-contractors.

60-hour working week — already a very feeble target.

Commenting on these shockingly poor results, the reports typically said:

"While our Code allows exceptions to work-hour standards in unusual or emergency circumstances, the practice of exceeding these limits appears to be routine rather than exceptional for some suppliers."

It is hard to imagine that Apple did not know about the grossly long hours that workers are forced to work by sub-contractors. Indeed, this factor has to be a key reason why they moved much of their production to countries such as China in the first place.

In the reports, Apple propose as a remedy such things as better management, and teaching workers that they have the right not to work more than 60 hours a week. But, given that the figures hardly improve up to 2012, it is clear these measures didn't make any impact and it is hard to believe that Apple cared very much about this.

What changed between 2012 and 2013 so that facilities making goods for Apple dramatically increased their compliance with Apple's target, from 38% to 92%? Well, first, we should caution against accepting the figures as accurate. But if anything improved at all in that time it was not that Apple suddenly got tough on their sub-contractors or had a fit of conscience and decided to take fewer profits from their business. No, the answer is that it was necessary to massage the figures to look better or even actually to improve conditions for workers on the ground because of increasing labour unrest in that period.

This unrest included mass strikes at the giant Foxconn complex where several brands manufacture goods, and the bad publicity the brands received as a result of worker suicides partly prompted by bad working conditions.

As a result of the outbreak of worker organising, in spring 2013 Foxconn workers won the right to elect representatives to negotiate for them with management, unprecedented in China and very rare in globalised industry.

We must support workers organising throughout globalised supply chains, from shopworkers in the UK to those making garments in Bangladesh, or electronic goods in China. No credence to Corporate Social Responsibility; maximum support for workers in struggle!

THE WELFARE STATE

BY CHARLOTTE ZALENS

The post-Second World War "welfare state" — more universal state schooling, the National Health Service, a comprehensive "safety net" benefits system — was a large concession to the working class. Measures which were calculated to head off post-war unrest, but also represented the culmination of working-class struggle. But as long as capitalism continued, the welfare state was always going to be vulnerable to erosion. Looking back over three decades since the rise of Thatcher and the brutal class ideology she represented the post-war "settlement" looks like an exceptional kind of capitalism. The welfare state has almost been obliterated.

What did the welfare state represent for women? It partially removed some of women's burden, increasingly a "double burden" as more women went into waged work.

For instance, state schools provided meals, medical inspections and longer hours of childcare. The benefits system staved off the deepest poverty. The health service ended the "doctor's pot", saving for medical emergencies, and drastically helped women overcome health problems associated with pregnancy and childbirth. It took some caring responsibilities away from women.

However, the welfare state still treated women as men's dependents. Underpinned by the National Insurance scheme, where better-off full-time workers put in more and got out more, women (who might be paid less, in part-time work, or taking breaks in work to bring up children) were often entitled to lower benefits and pensions. To a significant degree this inequality still stands.

But women still need a welfare state! At its best, the welfare state made abstract rights a practical reality for all women. The right to an abortion or to contraception becomes a practical reality when provided by a health service; not a matter of the ability to buy such services from private providers.

As socialists we should fight for and defend legal and political advances that subordinate the demands of profit to the needs of people. We should defend the legal rights and social gains we still have from further attack. That defence will bring wide layers of workers into a struggle to make their lives better, and to claw back ground from the ruling class.

Thatcher took on the welfare state and rolled back large sections of the gains the welfare state made for the working class. She was the first to really attempt this and did it wholesale, laying the ground for more to follow. New Labour took advantage of Thatcher's shock blow to the welfare state to continue to dismantle it. Since 2010 the Lib-Dem-Tory governments have not only built on New Labour's attacks, but used the financial crisis to go much further. There has been an escalation of the disintegration of the welfare state. Parts of it — the benefits system for instance — have been reduced to a safety net for "paupers".

The combined impact of welfare reforms since 2010 (to 2014 / 15) was calculated to be £14.9 billion, of which £11.1 billion will fall primarily on women. 74.5% of the burden of welfare cuts fall on women. The Tory government's attack on public sector pensions and the public sector pay freeze have disproportionately affected women as the majority of public sector workers are women. Job losses in the public sector — which will, if we cannot stop it, continue up to 2020 — have also therefore disproportionately effected women.

It is no coincidence that the public sector workforce has a majority of women because of the type of work that is available there. Fortunately decent pay, conditions and pensions made women workers lives better there. That is all now under threat.

Other attacks on the welfare state since 2010 have a heavy impact on women. The same House of Commons Library report shows that 60% of the burden of housing benefit reforms fall on women, 75% of the effect of tax credit changes, and 60% of the council tax benefit cut. In child benefit, 98% of the cuts' effect will fall on women. This is all on top of an increase in the cost of living that has not been met by an increase in wages, meaning a real terms wage cut.

The fight to defend the welfare state will also be a fight to defend jobs, wages and conditions of those who work in the welfare state. Unfortunately the big public sector unions failed to confront and defeat the attacks on public sector pensions, a key "austerity" measure of the government after 2010. That is why a fight to democratise and push for a militant, fighting politics within the labour movement — and at the same time to defend women workers — is essential.

VIOLENCE AGAINST WOMEN

BY CARMEN BASANT

In 2015 the United Nations ('Facts and Figures: Ending Violence Against Women') described the state of violence against women as a global pandemic, with 35% of women worldwide having experienced physical and/or sexual violence. Within this general picture, specific trends have been observed:

• Sixty-four million girls worldwide are child brides, with 46% of women in South Asia and 41% in West and Central Africa (aged between 20-24) married before the age of 18.

• Approximately 140 million girls and women worldwide have suffered female genital mutilation.

• Women and girls make up 55% of the estimated 20.9 million victims of forced labour worldwide, and 98% of the estimated 4.5 million that are forced into sexual exploitation.

• Rape is a pervasive tactic of repression in modern wars. For example, approximately 250,000-500,000 women and girls were raped during the 1994 Rwandan genocide.

In terms of geography, the World Health Organisation ('Global and regional estimates of violence against women', 2013) provides the following regional estimates: 29.8% of women in the Americas suffer violence from partners at some time in their lives; 25.4% in Europe; 24.6% in the Western Pacific; 36.6% in Africa; 37.0% in the Eastern Mediterranean; 37.7% in South-East Asia.

When analysing such statistics, one does need to factor in the relative social positioning of women across the world and the related likelihood of reporting instances of physical and sexual violence. This might explain why variation between regions is actually smaller than one might expect. Africa, the Eastern Mediterranean, and South-East Asia are discernable as particularly regressive regions vis-à-vis the abuse of women. This regional picture correlates with the World Economic Forum's regular indices of the global gender gap, which uses the development measures of health, education, economy and politics to map inequality between men and women.

THE CASE OF INDIA

The movement in India against sexual violence, which emerged from the end of 2012 onwards, is significant at both the national and global scale.

While rape in India is not new, what is new is the shifting social position of women. In urban India, new social relations and forces have arisen through the dialectical changes of capitalist globalisation, notably: the mass entry of women into the workforce, and a politicised, young, university-educated population. Such forces are violently colliding with the feudal survivals of religious, patriarchal culture.

In India after globalisation, cultural practices rooted in different eras can be found all in one place: son preference, under-age marriage, arranged marriage, dowry demands, gender unequal malnutrition, female foeticide, female infanticide, sex-trafficking, violence against women, rape. As the political activist Kavita Krishnan ('Capitalism, sexual violence and sexism') notes, "[c]aste oppression and patriarchal anxieties about marriage and dowry" mediate "the entry of women into the global labour market." In a piece in *The Hindu* newspaper, titled 'Rape and the crisis of Indian male masculinity', academic Ratna Kapur states:

"With the opening up of the market, women are more visible in the workplace. […] That they are entering male bastions of power has challenged the sense of superiority and entitlement of the traditional Indian male. This idea of a woman as a fully formed human subject remains a difficult concept to embrace […] Son preference simultaneously erodes the possibility of respect for women, as girls are seen as unwanted or burdensome. Such inequalities produce the very hatred against women in the public arena that we are witnessing throughout the country."

Kapur concludes, as "women assert their identity and enter his bastions of power, the traditional Indian male is reacting with violence".

FOUR CONCLUSIONS

1. There is global variation in the realities of capitalism and pre-capitalism, in how capitalism and patriarchy fuse and collide, and, more generally, in capitalist development. These conditions of existence shape and intersect with the social position of women and the phenomenon, degree and nature of violence against women around the world.

2. Capitalism is contradictory for women. It throws up openings — that, nonetheless, must be socially and politically hard fought for — alongside

SIMONE DE BEAUVOIR (1908-1986)

Born into a respectable, Parisian, middle-class family, de Beauvoir lived anything but a conventional life. She worked as a teacher in Rouen and later in Paris and wrote philosophy, novels and plays.

Her book *The Second Sex* (1949) explored the myths surrounding women in society, religion, literature and ideologies and strove to understand the reality that lay behind them. She did not claim there are no differences between men and women, but that the differences are constructed by society, not natural. Translated into many languages, The *Second Sex* has become essential reading for socialist women and men and was influential in the women's movements of the 60s and 70s.

De Beauvoir was ambivalent about activism — she was wary of political parties and believed being an intellectual was enough. However, she took strong public stands at times on particular issues. In the 1960s and 70s she formed an international "tribunal" condemning US involvement in Vietnam; signed a declaration attacking France's draconian anti-abortion laws with 342 other women; and was a leading figure in the French League of Women's Rights.

constraints — for example, in the commodification of women's bodies.

3. In an early Workers' Liberty pamphlet, *The Case for Socialist Feminism*, sexual violence is understood as an expression of men's declining relative power over women as a result of societal change.

In light of the specific case of India, and the wider picture of violence against women across the world, this conclusion retains much explanatory power:

"In truth, wider women's rights, increased circulation of pornography, and a growth in violent crime, including rape, are all based on one fundamental tendency — the break-up of old family structures, in an individualistic and competitive society where it is difficult to find alternatives to the family as a source of love and sympathy. The socialist answer is not to try to reimpose the old family structures, but to fight for a new society based on cooperation. […] Rape is violence, and not an exaggerated form of sex."

4. As summated by Kavita Krishnan (op cit.), for socialist feminists: "Locating the problem (and solution) of gender violence in moral values is more suited to a liberal analysis than a Marxist one. The struggle for women's emancipation, as understood by Marxists, has to be for a revolutionary transformation of the structure of production and reproduction. Socializing reproduction and getting rid of the gender division of labour must be key to such a transformation."

As Ellen Meiksins Wood notes, socialism "may not by itself guarantee the destruction of historical and cultural patterns of women's oppression", but "Socialism will be the first social form since the advent of class society whose reproduction as a social system is endangered rather than enhanced by relations and ideologies of domination and oppression.'" (From 'Capitalism and Human Emancipation: Race, Gender and Democracy' in *The Socialist Feminist Project: A Contemporary Reader in Theory and Politics*).

REFERENCES/FURTHER READING

Kavita Krishnan, Capitalism, sexual violence and sexism. Available at kafila.org/2013/05/23/capitalism-sexual-violence-and-sexism-kavita-krishnan/
Ratna Kupur, Rape and the crisis of Indian male masculinity. Available at www.thehindu.com/todays-paper/tp-opinion/rape-and-the-crisis-of-indian-masculinity/article4215421.ece
United Nations, Facts and Figures: Ending Violence against Women. Available at www.unwomen.org/en/what-we-do/ending-violence-against-women/facts-and-figures#notes
World Economic Forum, The Global Gender Gap Report 2015. Available at reports.weforum.org/global-gender-gap-report-2015/
World Health Organisation, Global and regional estimates of violence against women. Available at www.who.int/reproductivehealth/publications/violence/9789241564625/en
Workers' Liberty, *The Case for Socialist Feminism*. Available at womensfightback.wordpress.com/resources/the-case-for-socialist-feminism

The strike committee

THE MATCHWOMEN

The Bryant and May match factory in London's East End employed young (some as young as 13), mostly casual, mostly women workers. Many were from Irish immigrant families. They worked very long hours for poverty wages. On top of this they faced a punitive system of fines that pared their meagre wages down yet further; violence from the foremen; and the tedious, exhausting and downright dangerous nature of the work.

Conditions at the firm were exposed by the socialist H H Champion in the *Labour Elector*, by Tom Mann in an 1886 pamphlet arguing for the eight-hour day, and by Annie Besant in *The Link*. After Besant's article, Bryant and May threatened to sue for libel, and drafted a statement renouncing the article's claims, which they instructed the "matchgirls" to sign. The women refused; and the alleged ringleader was sacked, so the women in the department, and then in July 1888 the whole factory, walked out on strike.

There were mass meetings, collection and distribution of strike money, and widespread support from the young trade union movement. On 18 July, Bryant and May conceded all the women's demands. On 27 July, the workers set up the Union of Women Matchmakers.

The matchmakers' success was a turning point for the workers' movement — they were the sisters, mothers, daughters, wives and inspiration for other East End workers, like the gas workers and dockers who would strike a year later. Until then, many trade unionists had thought it not worthwhile to organise un-skilled workers.

The matchwomen sparked the "New Unionism" with the spread of organisa-tion and militancy among the previously unorganised.

THE FIGHT FOR REPRODUCTIVE FREEDOMS

BY ELLEN TRENT

The ability to control conception reliably, and deal with unwanted pregnancy, has been one of the most significant changes in the lives of many women — but sadly not all women — around the world.

In England and Wales two million women now take the pill, and an estimated 70% use it at some point in their lives; whilst around 200,000 women access safe abortion each year. We've also seen dramatic changes in attitudes towards sex and sexuality and to women's role in society more broadly. Women are having fewer children, or none at all, and more couples are co-habiting rather than marrying.

Most countries have liberalised their abortion laws to one degree or another. The United Nations (*Abortion Policies and Reproductive Health around the World*, 2013) report 97% of countries allow abortion to save a woman's life; 67% to preserve physical health; 63% to protect mental health; 49% permit abortion in cases of rape; and 29% of countries on the basis of a woman's request.

However, many countries still maintain highly restrictive abortion laws and formal legalisation can mask other barriers — gaps in implementation; lack of provision; mandatory and biased counselling; long waiting times; third-party consent; and high costs. These barriers are demeaning, undermine women's autonomy and are dangerous. Worldwide every year 21.6 million women have an unsafe abortion because they can't access safe care — 47,000 of those die (World Health Organisation, 'Safe and unsafe induced abortion', 2012).

Women in the UK still do not have "the right to choose". The 1967 Abortion Act, is limited and vulnerable to attack. Abortion is usually only available up to 24 weeks (already reduced from 28 weeks in 1990), has to be agreed by two doctors, and women must demonstrate that continuing the pregnancy would cause more harm than the termination. This process puts pressure on women to question their reasons and enables the doctors who are anti-choice to undermine and obstruct women's access to abortion.

Although Northern Ireland is part of the UK, the 1967 Act has never applied for women there. Abortion is still governed by the Offences Against the Person Act (1861) and the Criminal Justice Act (Northern Ireland) (1945) meaning abortion is only available where the pregnancy endangers the woman's life. The Family Planning Association estimates that around 2,000 women a year travel from Northern Ireland to England for an abortion but they do not have access to NHS services and so face costs ranging from £400-£2,000 on top of travel, accommodation, childcare, time off work and the difficulty of explaining to family where they are going.

Many women also travel each year from the Republic of Ireland where abortion law is highly restrictive. In 2013 the Protection of Life During Pregnancy Act finally introduced limited abortion rights, although only in cases where a woman's life is in danger or if she is suicidal and with many complicated processes.

This change came on the back of pressure following the death of Savita Halappanavar in 2012, who died of septicaemia after suffering a drawn-out miscarriage at 17-weeks pregnant. Doctors said they could not terminate the pregnancy and save her life because the foetus has a detectable heartbeat. This led to protests of thousands in Ireland, Britain, India and elsewhere calling for the government to legalise abortion.

In a society where we face judgements on our behaviour, clothes and sexual choices, women are still judged for having children at the "wrong time" or in the "wrong way" or not wanting to have children, and face increased judgement of over choices when pregnant — from drinking alcohol or coffee, to smoking, to the type of exercise we take or don't take, to driving a car! Women have to contend with social pressure around "acceptable" reasons to choose abortion, and expectations that we should feel sad or guilty about that choice.

If we choose to become parents we face pressure, whether subtly through media manipulation or overtly through a coercive benefits system, to comply with the shape of family that's most convenient for capitalism. Capitalism has adapted to accept same-sex parenting and marriage, yet LGBT parents and their children still face stigmatisation, as do solo parents.

Meanwhile, women, and our reproductive rights, are at the sharp end of the dismantling of the NHS and welfare state. The reality remains for many women, and most sharply for working-class women, that their financial independence decreases, or disappears, as soon as they have children due to the gender pay gap and soaring childcare costs. Attacks on the welfare state, such as benefit caps and cuts, reduce women's independence and often hit solo parents the hardest.

Privatisation and outsourcing open doors for anti-choice organisations to provide "NHS services" and sex and relationships education to young people. "Crisis Pregnancy Centres" run by right-wing Christian charities provide "advice to women" (i.e. lies) including about the link between abortion and increased risk of cancer; relationship breakdown; infertility; and increased risk of abusing children. More vulnerable women who are less familiar with the system, or more worried about talking to their family GP for privacy reasons (migrant or young women in particular) are more likely to find these centres on the internet and attend them. At the same time moves towards a "competitive health market" will make abortions more expensive, and commissioning services is unlikely to be a priority for the one quarter of GPs who are anti-choice.

We see a similar picture in sex and relationships education (SRE): the Tories have established a new forum to replace the Independent Advisory Group on Sexual Health and HIV — the Sex and Relationships Council. Anti-choice, religious organisations such as LIFE and Care Confidential were given seats on the council, yet the pro-choice British Pregnancy Advice Service was not re-offered a seat. Also included was The Silver Ring Thing which says it aims to bring "value-based, parent-centred" SRE providers to policy discussions.

Pro-choice activity in the UK has renewed in the last few years as a reaction to anti-choice organisations increasingly employing US-style intimidatory tactics outside abortion clinics; emotive pictures and arguments; lies about abortion; and harassing women entering clinics for advice and support. Local pro-choice groups, students and feminists have held counter-vigils outside clinics and developed support networks.

Initiated by anti-capitalist feminist group, Feminist Fightback, there has been an interesting debate about tactics. How can we effectively challenge anti-choicers? Is direct action appropriate when it often leads to violent clashes? What about legal challenges?[1]

There has also been a shift towards recognising the broad range of factors impacting on a woman's right and ability to choose, including economic and social pressures, and the different challenges facing women due to race, class, sexuality, disability and migration. There have also been interesting discussions around how to include trans* men in struggles (as they may still be affected by attacks on reproductive freedoms) without losing the analysis of limits on these rights as linked to gender inequality and women's oppression.

Unfortunately, there are also significant limits to the new pro-choice activity. In student unions there have been calls to simply ban anti-choice groups from campuses because they represent a "threat to women"; a better approach, one which would consolidate and build support, would be to mobilise and protest against anti-choice activities.

Most trade unions support reproductive freedoms, but they do little more than affiliate to the Abortion Rights Campaign Group.

Socialist and anti-capitalist feminists also face challenges in joining the dots between struggles — Abortion Rights is a single-issue campaign, seeking to build the "widest possible support", mainly to improve legal rights and access, with little to say on attacks to the welfare state or NHS.

If we are to really fight back against the attacks on our reproductive freedoms, pro-choice activity needs political ideas. What lessons can we learn from the history of the fight for reproductive freedoms? Does socialist feminism have anything unique to say about this fight? We will explore those questions in the following pages.

A HISTORY OF THE FIGHT FOR REPRODUCTIVE FREEDOMS

THE BIRTH CONTROL MOVEMENT

In the early 20th century arguments for birth control were more widely taken up in the UK, although for a variety of motivations. The ruling class wanted to prevent the "unfit working-classes" reproducing; the Malthusian League thought birth control could "cure" poverty which they believed was caused by overpopulation. But some on the left argued on the basis of the right to knowledge or a woman's right to control her body.

Campaigners in the UK were influenced by women in the US such as Margaret Sanger who founded the first birth control clinic and wrote the pamphlet *Family Limitation* (1915) or revolutionary socialist Antoinette Konikow's *Voluntary Motherhood* (1923). In the UK Marie Stopes published *Married Love* (1918) and *Wise Parenthood* (1918) and in 1921 Stopes opened the first clinic in the UK. Throughout the 1920s and 1930s clinics opened across the country. Some were motivated by Malthusian and eugenicist ideas, but others were established by socialists and feminists with funds from local trade union branches.

Socialist feminist Stella Browne campaigned for birth control, abortion and divorce rights before the First World War and through the 1920s and 30s. Browne was influenced by the growing movement linking feminism, gay liberation and socialism in Europe, and was excited by the work of Bolshevik, Alexandra Kollontai and others in Russia.

After the October Revolution in 1917 women's reproductive rights were amongst the first legal changes made by the Bolsheviks in Russia; they tried to establish provision of childcare, birth control and legalised abortion, and proper training for doctors and midwives, although these were limited by civil war conditions. Discussions raged on sexual relationships and the nature of the family.

Browne based her arguments on the immediate needs of working-class women and on the socialist commitment to equality between men and women which was impossible if women could not control reproduction. She joined up the dots between birth control and abortion and housing, education and unemployment, in thinking about a woman's right to choose. Throughout the 1920s Browne travelled around the country speaking to packed meetings about reproductive freedoms. The women (and men) in attendance were gripped with interest and hopeful about the change birth control could bring.

Browne was part of a new feminism which wanted women not only to be able to access the "men's world" (work, education, the vote) but to highlight that real equality required recognising women's specific challenges (domestic labour, reproduction, etc). They fought more traditional feminists who saw sex simply as a male imposition on women. However, even amongst these new feminists, Browne and other socialist feminists were "remarkable in not isolating birth control but in continuing to make connections between sexual politics and socialism in the 1920s and 30s" (Sheila Rowbotham, *A new world for women: Stella Browne, socialist feminist*, 1977). Others, lacking an analysis of capitalism, often fell into traditional ideas about women's "natural" role.

The birth control movement slowly made ground but women were still being criminalised for, and dying from, unsafe abortions. The 1861 Offences Against the Person Act made abortion illegal and women had to resort to taking poison or inserting knitting needles and hair pins into their uteruses.

In 1936 Browne, alongside Janet Chance, Dora Russell and Alice Jenkins, established the Abortion Law Reform Association (ALRA) — building its membership rapidly through women's branches of the co-operative movement. 1938 saw a landmark trial when a Dr Aleck Bourne was acquitted for performing an abortion on a 14-year-old rape victim — after this the prosecution had to prove that a doctor had not acted for the patient's welfare, but it remained very difficult for women to access abortion.

Browne stood in a long tradition of socialists and feminists exploring the relationship between equality and women's ability to control reproduction. Some of the early utopian socialist communities practiced contraception and free unions, arguing that "free love" was the necessary basis of a free society. Engels and Bebel explored the way in which class society and capitalism shaped sexuality and sexual relationship. In *The Woman Question* (1886) Eleanor Marx discussed double standards in attitudes towards sex, adultery and divorce and argued for the importance of sex education and understanding consent.

However, despite this, women like Browne had to struggle within the left and labour movement for reproductive freedoms to be taken seriously. Some suspicion resulted from the relationship between eugenicists and the birth control movement. Others dismissed the question as irrelevant to politics; reformist Labour leaders acted to defend traditional ideas of the family; and economic determinists thought birth control was an individual matter as any sexual oppression would end automatically with the end of capitalism. Browne met this response from a male comrade when she was in the Communist Party (CP):

"[O]n the subject of sex equality, the majority of my women comrades are as unsound as their capitalist-minded sisters. It is time that some of our sex-obsessed comrades realised that woman's so-called slavery to man is solely owing to her economic dependence on him and can only end when the capitalist regime ends" (*The Communist*, 26 August 1922, in Rowbotham op cit.)

The CP refused to have a position on birth control and abortion until the mid-1920s (then supporting it on the basis of women being able to fully participate in the struggle). Finding no space for her ideas or debate, Browne left the CP in 1923.

Alongside socialist Dora Russell she took the fight into the Labour Party, forming the Workers' Birth Control Group in 1924 to campaign within the labour, socialist and co-operative movements. They joined forces with socialist women and men and were explicitly opposed to eugenicism, arguing that all women have an equal right to knowledge, and that the state should be responsible for provision. Unfortunately, they faced many of the old arguments and motions to Labour Party conference were narrowly defeated, or, if they passed, forgotten by the leadership.

Towards the end of the 1920s and into the 1930s, the movement for reproductive freedoms and its link with the left and labour movement weakened. Socialist feminists like Browne continued to fight but feminism became more liberal as capitalism adapted to accommodate some feminist ideas about sex and reproduction, although it maintained the sexual division of labour and the traditional structure of the family. At the same time, socialist feminism became more marginal as the impact of Stalinism, the economic crisis and the rise of fascism narrowed the opportunities for discussion of sexual and personal liberation.

THE SEXUAL REVOLUTION

In the 1960s technological and medical developments, growing concerns around the high number of maternal deaths due to unsafe abortion and pressure of the burgeoning women's movement, combined to create leaps forward for reproductive freedoms.

The pill became widely available in 1961 (available for single women in 1967 and free of charge from 1974) and in 1967 the Abortion Act passed. After this success, reproductive freedoms were not expected to continue to be a major focus for struggle. However, dissatisfied anti-choice campaigners began to step up

---

SYLVIA PANKHURST (1882-1960)

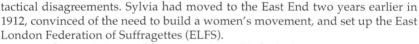

Sylvia Pankhurst was a socialist feminist, who during the campaign for women's suffrage at the turn of the 20th century, not only braved the horrors of hunger striking and forcible feeding, but also founded and built a remarkable women's organisation in London's East End.

She was involved in the Women's Social and Political Union's (WSPU) militant activities from the start — organising in London from 1906 alongside Annie Kenney and Marxist Feminist Dora Montefiore (a member of the Social Democratic Federation and later founder member of the Communist Party in 1920).

Sylvia was expelled from the WSPU in 1914 by her mother and sister, Emmeline and Christabel, over tactical disagreements. Sylvia had moved to the East End two years earlier in 1912, convinced of the need to build a women's movement, and set up the East London Federation of Suffragettes (ELFS).

In March 1914 Sylvia and her comrades published *The Women's Dreadnought* paper (*Workers' Dreadnought* from 1917) which Sylvia organised until 1924. It reported on the struggles for suffrage, labour struggles and women's life experiences. Sylvia saw the *Dreadnought* as being "…a medium through which working women, however unlettered, might express themselves, and find their interests defended."

Alongside this the ELFS organised marches and demonstrations for a woman's right to vote, calling for equal pay for equal work, and an end to the "sweating trades" — mobilising thousands of women and men.

Although she drifted from independent working class politics, Sylvia remained a committed anti-racist and anti-fascist and continued to fight for maternity rights and better conditions for working-class women and children until her death.

activity; in response, second-wave feminism explicitly posed abortion as a women's rights issue.

Free contraception, abortion on demand, and free 24-hour childcare provision were among the founding demands of the women's liberation movement in 1970 and, throughout the decade, campaigns formed of elements from the women's movement, the extra-parliamentary socialist left and the labour movement to fight to defend and extend the 1967 Act. The most significant was the National Abortion Campaign (NAC), formed in 1975 in response to an attempt to restrict the law introduced into Parliament by James White a Labour MP; his Bill aimed to restrict the reasons women could have abortions and which doctors could perform one.

NAC opposed any steps back from the current law but also rejected the familial ideology underpinning the 1967 Abortion Act and actively challenged the authority of the state to govern women's choices at all. They linked the fight for reproductive freedoms to a critique of the family, to the fight for women to avoid dependency on men, and to the freeing of women's sexuality.

White's bill was defeated but was followed by the Benyon Bill in 1977 and the 1979 Corrie Bill which aimed to drastically reduce time limits and restrict the grounds for abortion. NAC organised large demonstrations against the bills and lobbied Labour MPs, including working with the Campaign Against the Corrie Bill (CACB) and the TUC in October 1979 to organise the largest pro-choice demonstration ever held in Britain, with more than 60,000 people marching.

The labour movement and a working alliance with organisations such as the TUC provided the necessary ally for a broad based, national campaign, especially as the women's movement had no comparable structures, organisation, influence or membership. It was also a way to relate to, and work with, the rising numbers of women trade unionists who were central to pushing the pro-choice agenda in unions.

But, whilst NAC continued to argue for free abortion on demand, it also had to compromise, as neither the trade union movement or the Labour Party wanted to call for a woman's right for abortion on demand — the TUC slogan was "keep it legal, keep it safe" (Lesley Hoggart, 'Feminist Principles meet Political Reality'). NAC also faced continued hostility toward feminism that existed in pockets of the labour movement. Given this, NAC's success in mobilising trade union support for abortion rights was impressive. They attempted to navigate the compromise with a hierarchy of demands ranging from a feminist critique of the 1967 Act, on the basis that it was not premised on a woman's right to choose; through a criticism of the rights within the act and a fight to improve access to abortion; to activity to defend the 1967 Act against further restrictions. They formed broader campaigns with allies (such as CACB) to allow them to raise the different levels of political demands at the same time, under different banners.

However, tensions developed within NAC around strategy, structures and compromise. Socialist feminists argued that NAC should continue to advocate for a woman's right to choose but that working with the labour movement remained vital for reaching out to working-class women:

"When the women's movement has the opportunity to drag the labour movement behind it in defence of a hard won step forward for women's liberation — then it must obviously be grabbed with all hands and feet" (NAC News in Hoggart, op cit.).

Radical feminists criticised NAC for "concentrating its energies too much on the male bureaucracies of the unions rather than the women at the grass-roots" and argued strongly for women-only campaigning, and grassroots consciousness-raising groups. These feminists split after the 1979 demo to create the Abortion Action Group.

NAC continued to fight throughout the 1980s and 1990s, including arguing for improved abortion rights (unsuccessfully) and attempts to reverse the "Gillick Ruling", a High Court judgement which ruled under-16s could be prescribed contraceptives without their parents' knowledge (successfully). However, unfortunately, the campaign, like many others, suffered from a lack of energy and de-politicisation, from the decline in the women's movement and the defeats of the labour movement in the 1980s. In 2003 NAC merged with the Abortion Law Reform Association to form Abortion Rights.

ANTOINETTE KONIKOW (1869-1946)

Antoinette Konikow was a founder of the communist and Trotskyist movements in the USA. She was a medical doctor and one of the key campaigners for women's reproductive freedoms in the USA.

Born in the Russian Empire, Konikow attended university in Zurich where she became politically active, joining Plekhanov's Emancipation of Labour Group — the first Russian Marxist Group. She moved to America in 1893 and almost immediately joined the Socialist Labor Party of America (SLP). She went on to become a founder member of the Socialist Party of America, Communist Party USA, and the Communist League of America. She was an outspoken supporter of the ideas of Leon Trotsky, against Joseph Stalin, and remained active in the American Trotskyist movement until the end of her life.

As a physician and a feminist, Konikow was committed to the then-taboo cause of birth control. She was a member of the Society of Sanitary and Moral Prophylaxis and, along with her son-in-law Joseph Vanzler (later active as a Trotskyist under the name John G Wright), she developed an inexpensive contraceptive which she shared with Soviet officials on a visit to Russia as a birth control specialist in 1926. Konikow's 1923 book, *Voluntary Motherhood*, is regarded as a seminal work in the history of 20th century American feminism.

REPRODUCTIVE FREEDOMS AND SOCIALIST FEMINISM

The history of the fight for reproductive freedoms highlights differences of ideas, motivation and tactics but also the importance of debating these in order to fight together.

Many pro-choice activists today rely on the argument that there is now a "pro-choice majority" (Abortion Rights puts this as high as 76%) and that the law should come into line with public opinion. The problem with this is that it is limited (legal changes will not address the broad range of factors which work to limit our right to choose) and, importantly, patches over disagreements. There are gaps and differences within that 76%, especially around later abortion or women's reasons for wanting an abortion and there are tactical disagreements about how to fight for reproductive freedoms. It also misses the point, that women would be able to control our bodies, irrespective of public opinion.

Stella Browne advocated for abortion rights from 1915 but was in a minority initially — others felt that fighting for abortion would divert attention from birth control campaigns, which were more immediately winnable. Browne was willing to work with the majority (whilst opposing any attempts to increase the harsh punishments for abortion) but on the basis that she continued to argue for the inclusion of the fight for abortion rights. This lesson came through again as NAC navigated maintaining the fight for free abortion on demand with the need to build unity with the broader labour movement, that could make having and winning that fight a reality.

We should look for opportunities to discuss tactics with others, including the lessons we can learn from sisters fighting to defend and extend reproductive freedoms around the world, as well as the lessons we can learn from history. We can, and should, fight in broader alliances — these will throw up contradictions, questions and compromises and we should be open to exploring and debating these.

Reproductive freedoms cannot be a single-issue campaign — we have to join the dots.

Socialist feminists see the right to control our bodies as a fundamental human right. It is an issue for everyone, but is especially important for working-class women who may lack the resources to deal with unplanned pregnancy or other pressures. If we recognise that the "right to choose" is affected by a broad range of issues (from sex and relationships education; access to contraception and abortion; availability of good quality healthcare; maternity rights; benefits; childcare; support for parents; social attitudes and more) then the fight for reproductive freedoms is not, and cannot be, a single-issue or apolitical campaign. We need to work to integrate arguments around attacks on the NHS and welfare state into reproductive justice demands, and vice versa.

Socialist feminists also understand that there is a relationship between reproductive freedoms and the kind of world we live in. True reproductive freedom is impossible in a society based on inequality and exploitation. We should fight for reforms under capitalism, but these will be limited and will always put the needs of the state and ruling class before women's freedom. Women like Stella Browne fought to raise the revolutionary role and potential of reproductive freedoms and were clear that they were not a way of making the current system work better.

Our demand for reproductive freedoms sits alongside our critique of the way the family unit functions under capitalism and the role women play in providing free labour (cooking, cleaning and caring) so that the working class stays alive to turn up to work, day after day, generation after generation. It sits alongside our critique of the way capitalism and class society constrain the potential of human relationships. It is a fight to dismantle the ideas and stereotypes about women and gender which have grown up around the way capitalism uses and relies on women's reproductive capacities — to separate sex and reproduction and raise the question of women's sexuality and sexual enjoyment.

On the other hand, fighting for, and winning, reproductive freedoms is central to making not only women's liberation but working-class liberation possible. The ability to choose whether and when to have children is central to women's ability to make real choices about life and work; to increasing our independence; and to facilitating our involvement in struggle and the labour movement, without which a revolution to create a new society will be impossible. This is why Stella Browne saw reproductive freedoms as "the key to a new world for women" (Stella Browne, *The right to abortion*).

REFERENCES AND FURTHER READING

Feminist Fightback collective (2013) 'Anti-Choice Vigils: a debate on tactics' (bit.ly / FF-tactics)

Feminist Fightback collective (2015) 'Fighting for reproductive justice' (bit.ly / FF-reproductivejustice)

Lesley Hoggart, 'Feminist Principles meet Political Reality'. Available at www.prochoiceforum.org.uk / al6.php

Sheila Rowbotham (1977) *A New World for Women: Stella Browne, Socialist Feminist*

United Nations, Abortion Policies and Reproductive Health around the World. Available at www.un.org / en / development / desa / population / publications / pdf / policy / AbortionPoliciesReproductiveHealth.pdf

Rosie Woods (2013) 'Why we defend abortion rights' *Women's' Fightback* (bit.ly / abortion-rights)

World Health Organisation, Safe and unsafe induced abortion — Global and regional levels in 2008, and trends during 1995–2008. Available at www.who.int / reproductivehealth / publications / unsafe_abortion / rhr_12_02 / en /

WOMEN, SOCIALISM AND RELIGION

BY ELIZABETH BUTTERWORTH

"I have endeavoured to dissipate these religious superstitions from the minds of women, and base their faith on science and reason, where I found for myself at least that peace and comfort I could never find in the Bible and the church. . . the less they believe, the better for their own happiness and development. . . ."
Elizabeth Cady Stanton, *The Degraded Status of Women in the Bible*

It is clear from even a brief scan of the news that much religion has an oppressive agenda; whether it's from the Catholic Church in Ireland, opposing the rights of same-sex couples to marry or adopt; the Bodu Bala Sena (BBS, meaning "Buddhist Power Force") in Sri Lanka, attacking the rights of non-Sinhalese ethnic groups; religious justification for the treatment of lower castes in India; Jewish Orthodox rabbis in London telling women that they shouldn't drive; or rampaging, misogynist, imperialist violence from Islamists such as the Islamic State (Daesh), Ansar Dine and Boko Haram.

Having said that, there are examples in every major religion of reformers, of progressives, but secularists push forward and, in general, it is religion that is catching up. This is especially the case with LGBT (lesbian, gay, bisexual and trans) rights, and abortion rights. The Bishop of Dublin even admitted recently that the Catholic Church is falling behind the rest of Irish society. It looks archaic.

Better religious people would tell me that, overall, religion has a positive effect on the world and that I'm just picking the worst parts. I could write about Solidarnosc (the Polish trade union and social movement that fought Stalinism and had links to the Catholic Church), or some of the liberation theologians, or feminist Islam? Of course, many atheists and secularists also leave a lot to be desired in terms of their actions and behaviour. But, as well as the numerous examples of horrendous reaction among major religions, it's also very hard to make a positive case for religion being in any way necessary.

Can we not use the skills we have and our brains to make the world a better place, without religion getting in the way? Or perhaps, if you think some religious teaching has some use or positives, taking these parts and leaving behind the rest? People should not need the incentive of religion to be decent.

The typical arguments put forward are: That religion helps people to empathise. That some religious groups promote peace and understanding. That religion is a basic human need. That religion helps people with their lives. There is a lack of logic to these arguments though. The implication is that atheists are less capable of doing these, or that some people need religion as a crutch. It's an underestimation of human beings to suggest that we need religion. We have reason, we have science, we have philosophy; we do not need religion to make sense of the world.

WHERE RELIGION COMES FROM

One of the most common explanations for the existence of religion, in sociological and anthropological terms, is that religion is a creation of the society it exists in. Stewart Elliott Guthrie writes, in a chapter called 'Projection' in *Guide to the Study of Religion*:

"The view that religion is, in some sense, a casting of human qualities upon the nonhuman world may be old as well as popular. Thornton says that it began at least with Herodotus and continued with Lucretius and Spinoza. Others point to Xenophanes's famous remark that if lions and horses could represent their gods, these gods would look like lions and horses. Certainly Spinoza (1955) and Hume (1957 [1757]) argued that popular religion, at least, is a product of human experience and an objectification of human needs and desires."

The idea of projection is made in Feuerbach's important book *The Essence of Christianity*, which was influential upon many thinkers including Marx and Engels. Feuerbach, inverting Hegel's ideas about the self-realisation of the divine through nature, argued that religious ideas were "involuntary projections of the essential attributes of human nature" (V A Harvey, *Feuerbach and the Interpretation of Religion*).

Another very common point is that religion creates order where there is seeming disorder and helps to explain the world around us. In terms of explaining the world around us, the abundance of creation myths in all sorts of religions would suggest that human beings want to understand where the world and universe came from, though arguably this is becoming more irrelevant the more we can use science to explain this.

Marx was also a projectionist, arguing that "man makes religion" and saw religion as something that both made people happy and miserable: the "heart in a heartless world". It is worth reading the whole text of the 1843 article *Critique of Hegel's Philosophy of Right* for Marx's views on where religion comes from. The "opium" that Marx compares religion to is not an allusion to religion as a universally evil force, but as a multi-faceted phenomenon that causes suffering, relieves suffering and that humans can shake off.

IS RELIGION STILL IMPORTANT?

In contemporary sociology, one of the biggest debates is and has been regarding secularisation theory, particularly since Bryan Wilson argued (*Religion in Sociological Perspective*) that non-scientific systems are engaged in an irreversible decline, as well as the publication of Steve Bruce's boldly-titled 2002 book *God is Dead: Secularization in the West*, in which the basic argument is that religion in the west is in terminal decline. There is some truth in this. Agnostics and atheists, if taken together, now make up 16% of the population of the USA. The membership and attendance of the big Protestant churches in Britain is plummeting, especially the Church of England, the Church of Scotland, and the Methodist Church: it would take a miracle to revive these. Michael Rosie's article 'Death by Committee' (2002) in *Theology in Scotland* (6) is a particularly good case study. There are also countries in which most people are atheist or agnostic: for example the Czech Republic, Sweden, the Netherlands, and arguably, Japan and China.

However, 84% of the world's adults are still religious. Certain forms of religion have grown, such as those defined as New Religious Movements, a more fluid, "pick-and-mix" approach to religion and superstition; and religious fundamentalism may be on the rise. Gita Saghal and Nira Yuval-Davis (in *Refusing Holy Orders*) point out a number of fundamentalist religious movements claiming theirs is the only true version of their religion, aiming to maintain tradition (orthodox), and looking to return to the truth (revivalist). Further, these movements seek to impose their version of religion via political means, perhaps through merging religion and the state; and tend to be patriarchal. They point out fundamentalist movements in all major religions, including the Hindu Right in India, which seeks to impose a Hindu state; and to groups of fundamentalist Jews who wish to impose a theocratic state in Israel; as well as the more well-publicised Christian and Muslim fundamentalist groups.

MARXIST ATTITUDES TOWARDS RELIGION

As pointed out earlier, Marx was a projectionist and agreed with Feuerbach that humans make religion. He staunchly defended the right to criticise religion and linked rejection of religion to the liberation of humankind, writing, "The abolition of religion as the illusory happiness of the people is the demand for their real happiness. To call on them to give up their illusions about their condition is to call on them to give up a condition that requires illusions. The criticism of religion is, therefore, in embryo, the criticism of that vale of tears of which religion is the halo. Criticism has plucked the imaginary flowers on the chain not in order that man shall continue to bear that chain without fantasy or consolation, but so that he shall throw off the chain and pluck the living flower" (Karl Marx, Critique of Hegel's Philos*ophy of Right*). Engels argued in *A Communist Confession of Faith* (1847) that religion would no longer be necessary in communism, as religion is linked to a historical stage — communism "makes [religions] superfluous and supersedes them".

It is both possible and necessary to have extremely disparaging views about religion, as Marx and Engels did, and yet think that some religious groups are the subject of intense, immoral persecution, and, furthermore, that the right to practising religion must be defended. It's unequivocally true that various religious groups around the world and in Britain face intense and horrific persecution. In London, mosques and synagogues have been attacked by fascists.

It is also true to say that the British left's view of religion has become seriously disoriented. Most of the time, the left stays silent on religion, shying away from getting into arguments with people about deeply held personal beliefs, and perhaps thinking that people will eventually shed these views if we can convince them of socialism.

Sometimes, the left strays into apologism for religious reaction of the worst kinds, such as supporting the Iranian regime's initiatives (see Workers' Liberty 'The SWP's double standards'), and working with the Muslim Brotherhood (see Workers' Liberty, 'Shelving socialism: the launch of Respect'). It shouldn't be necessary to argue why this is "bad" from both a socialist and feminist standpoint. At the very least, it is unprincipled to "lash up" with any religious group if it involves setting aside criticisms. But worse, parts of the mainstream left have made excuses for fundamentalist religion, which is nearly always deeply misogynistic.

Fundamentalist religion enforces traditional gender roles, emphasising the importance of women's purity and shaming us, justifying its actions with holy books, doctrine and demagogic leaders. It is not interested in the working class other than as a tool.

FEMINIST ATTITUDES

If you were to read an A-level sociology textbook, the impression you would get of feminist attitudes towards religion is that feminism is hostile to religion; that radical (and some liberal) feminists think religion is patriarchal; and Marxist feminists are opposed to religion as both an oppressive institution and as an irrational waste of time. In 1885, Elizabeth Cady Stanton wrote, "History shows us that the moral degradation of woman is due more to theological superstitions than to all other influences together." I would be inclined to agree with her, although I believe that class society and capitalism are obviously huge sources of oppression for women and have been for hundreds of years. The work of Women Against Fundamentalism and Southall Black Sisters has been an inspiring source of secularist feminism, especially SBS's recent defence of Charlie Hebdo staff, murdered in 2015, while much of the left and the feminist movement was clamouring to condemn them. There are other examples of principled secularist feminism.

Unfortunately, there is also a strong tradition in feminism of trying to "reclaim" religion; attempting to make religion more woman-centric; as well as spiritualist effluent about a mother God, sometimes linked to eco-feminism. For example, this quote from Alice Walker's *The Color Purple*:

"What do it look like? I ast.

"Don't look like nothing, she say. It ain't a picture show. It ain't something you can look at apart from anything else, including yourself. I believe God is everything, say Shug. Everything that is or ever will be. And when you can feel that, and be happy to feel that, you've found It."

The key to our liberation as working class women is being able to use reason to overcome the prevailing sexist, classist culture that tries to tell us that we are worthless. While it's obviously possible to use reason and be religious, superstition asks us to suspend disbelief and to stop thinking.

As socialist feminists, we should be for the right to practise religion without the interference of the state. We should also be against state religion and state endorsement of religion and thus for secularism. Religion is made by humans and used by humans. In most forms it is also heavily patriarchal, often more viciously than the rest of society. We should reject it as it is irrational, and criticise its various shortcomings, including its holy books, its priests and prophets.

REFERENCES AND FURTHER READING

Steve Bruce (2002), *God is Dead: Secularisation in the West*.
Stewart Elliott Guthrie in *Guide to the Study of Religion*, eds. Willi Braun, Russell T McCutcheon (2000).
Frederick Engels, A Communist Confession of Faith. Available at www.marxists.org/archive/marx/works/1847/06/09.htm

Paul Hampton (2006). 'The Truth about Marxism and Religion'. Available at www.workersliberty.org/node/5953

V A Harvey (1995), *Feuerbach and the Interpretation of Religion.*

Karl Marx, *Critique of Hegel's Philosophy of the Right'*. Available at www.marxists.org/archive/marx/works/1843/critique-hpr/

Elizabeth Cady Stanton, 'Has Christianity Benefited Woman?' in *Elizabeth Cady Stanton: Feminist As Thinker*, ed. Ellen Carol DuBois and Richard Candida Smith (2007).

Michael Rosie, 'Death by Committee', *Theology in Scotland* IX (2).

Gita Saghal and Nira Yuval-Davis (eds.) (1992), *Refusing holy orders: women and fundamentalism in Britain.*

Southall Black Sisters, 'We are Charlie'. Available at www.southallblacksisters.org.uk/we-are-charlie/

Martin Thomas (2013), 'Marxists and religion: the left is seriously disoriented'. Available at www.workersliberty.org/story/2013/10/22/marxists-and-religion-left-seriously-disoriented

Alice Walker (1982), *The Color Purple.*

Bryan Wilson (1984), *Religion in Sociological Perspective.*

Workers' Liberty, 'The SWP's double standards on religion'. Available at: www.workersliberty.org/story/2010/10/04/richard-dawkins-pope-and-al-quds-swps-double-standards-religion

Workers' Liberty, 'Shelving socialism: the launch of Respect'. Available at www.workersliberty.org/node/1612

THE GERMAN SOCIAL-DEMOCRATIC WOMEN'S MOVEMENT

BY JESSICA BRADWELL

During the 19th century, the emerging workers' movement began to develop its policy on the "woman question". On the one hand, early utopian socialists such as Charles Fourier argued strongly for the equality of women with men. On the other hand, Ferdinand Lassalle led the "proletarian anti-feminists", opposing votes for women and urging male workers to strike against women's entry into industrial labour. Marxists opposed Lassalle, arguing that women's participation in waged work was a step forward, taking her out of the private sphere and isolated domestic drudgery of the family household. It was a precondition for liberation.

In 1875, the Socialist Labour Party of Germany — later to become the Social Democratic Party (SPD) — was formed. In 1879, imprisoned SPD leader August Bebel published *Women and Socialism*. The book had an enormous impact, awakening both women and men to the potential of working-class women. In 1890, Germany's Anti-Socialist Law, which forbade socialists from organising, was repealed.

The stage was now set for the appearance of a landmark working-class women's movement, led by Clara Zetkin. It was to mobilise thousands of women, and make a great contribution to socialist theory and practice on women's liberation. How did they do that?

German socialist women placed strong emphasis on education. They set up education clubs for women and girls (Frauen- and Madchen-Bildungsverein), which held meetings, hosted lectures, published articles and pamphlets, and gathered information on women's working conditions. Each club had between 50 and 250 members, who paid a small monthly fee.

By 1905, 3,000 women were members of education clubs. From 1908, women's reading evenings (Leseabende) operated in around 150 localities, by 1910 involving 4,000 women. A women's library (Frauenbibliotek) collected speeches, pamphlets and reprints of newspaper articles.

Most of the leading socialist women — Luise Zietz, Clara Zetkin, Ottilie Baader — were involved in educating other women. And most of the socialist movement's female public speakers had gained their knowledge, understanding and confidence through socialist women's education.

In August 1889, a meeting in Berlin founded a women's agitation commission (Frauen-Agitationkommission) to co-ordinate political work amongst women. Commissions were formed in other towns, and set about recruiting women to the SPD and the trade unions, and convincing socialist men to support the women's cause. They ran speaker tours, produced literature, and campaigned on issues of interest to working women.

The membership of each commission was limited to three, in an attempt to avoid state persecution. However, after persistent state harassment, the agitation commissions were banned in 1895.

The Anti-Socialist Law banned only political combination, not the activities of individuals. So the socialist women passed the commissions' role to individual women organisers, Vertrauenspersonen. Their work was co-ordinated by a Zentralvertrauensperson — Ottilie Gerndt from 1895; Ottilie Baader from 1899. In 1900, the Party voted to include the women organisers in its formal structures, and, from 1904, paid the central organiser a wage. By 1907, there were 407 women organisers.

Continuing industrialisation in Germany meant that by 1892 there were six million women in the workforce. Only 5,000, though, were members of the free trade unions. In 1894, the SPD produced a plan for a unionisation drive among working women, including appointing women to union positions, and special lectures for working women. Within two years, women's union membership had risen to more than 12,000.

In 1896, 10,000 garment workers held a major strike, centred in Berlin. Their demands included: fixed wage scales; prompt delivery of materials and collection of finished products; weekly payment of wages; the establishment of arbitration boards; and, most important, replacing homeworking with factory-like workshops (Betriebwerkstatten). The socialist women supported the strike by monitoring working conditions; holding mass meetings in Berlin; collecting money for the strike fund; and providing extensive coverage in *Die Gleichheit*.

Despite the unionisation efforts, the majority of the women recruited to the socialist movement were the wives of men already active in the SPD.

The Party's women's congress in Berlin in 1913 addressed this, holding a special session on "How do we recruit unmarried women workers?" The opening speaker noted that:

"For the most part it is only the wives of our comrades who belong to the party organisation. The great mass of female industrial workers is still lacking. I think we've been somewhat remiss in directing our women's recruitment efforts too much at women in their role as housewives and mothers... We don't have material for agitation among unmarried woman workers."

Richard Evans — a leading historian of the German socialist women's movement — argues that the fact that the majority of socialist women were the wives of socialist men "contradicted the ideology of the SPD by disproving the theory of direct mobilisation through factory work". The SPD's policy followed Engels' and Bebel's line of argument: women's labour was a progressive development, primarily because it encouraged women to take part in working-class struggle alongside men.

Evans' mistake is to interpret this as an immediate effect on individual women. He sees the SPD's theory as meaning that the trend for women to work in factories would politicise only those women working in factories. It is more likely that industrialisation would affect working-class women's consciousness and mobilisation in a more general, collective way. Simply because a working-class woman did not, at a given time, undertake factory labour, did not mean that industrialisation did not affect her. Women as housewives and mothers felt the effects of prices, taxes, wages and social provision. The economic and political world deeply affects personal lives.

From the early 1890s, leading socialist women had put forward the idea of socialist women's congresses. Beginning in 1893, women delegates held meetings at Party congresses. Twenty women attended the first official German socialist women's congress in 1900, and discussed extending the system of women organisers, agitation among women workers, and the attitude that socialist women should take to the bourgeois women's movement. Women's congresses were held every two years after that, and grew steadily: 74 women attended the event in 1908.

In 1890, the Party founded a women's newspaper, *Die Arbeiterin* (*The Woman Worker*). A year later, Clara Zetkin took over as editor. The paper's name was changed to *Die Gleichheit* (*Equality*), subtitled "for the interest of the woman worker". With Zetkin as editor for the next 25 years, it was by far the most important publication for German socialist women.

Die Gleichheit's aims were: to provide material for socialist women agitators; to heighten the political consciousness of working-class women; to intensify class struggle by sharpening class differences; and to act as a communication channel.

CLARA ZETKIN (1857-1933)

Clara Zetkin pioneered the idea of a working-class women's movement. In 1891 she became editor of the German Social-Democratic Party (SPD) women's newspaper, *Die Gleichheit* (*Equality*), which she produced for 25 years. She became the secretary of the International Socialist Women in 1910 and was one of the founders of International Working Women's Day, which is still observed around the world today.

Zetkin advocated economic independence for women workers, arguing for the right to equal wages, for union representation and state-funded childcare. She fought for equal political rights, such as the right to vote; advocated the right to divorce and to abortion; and analysed the role of the family in women's oppression.

By 1910 there were 189,442 women in trade unions, 82,642 women members of the SPD, and *Die Gleichheit* had a circulation of 82,000 — which peaked in 1913 at 112,000. Zetkin and others she organised with firmly identified themselves as a movement for working-class women, distinct from the "bourgeois feminists" of the time. Zetkin argued that women of the capitalist class and women of the working class were engaged in struggles for a different kind of liberation. Bourgeois women sought to the right to compete with men of their own class on a "level playing field". Working-class women were part of a struggle alongside men of their own class to abolish class society and liberate humanity.

Zetkin was consistently on the left of the SPD. With Rosa Luxemburg and others she opposed World War One and went on to found the German Communist Party.

It included a regular column, "The Working Women's Movement" (Arbeiterinnen-Bewegung), a noticeboard for meetings and events. The paper published reports on women's working conditions, and information on employment legislation, so that women could exercise their (limited) legal rights. There was supportive coverage of working women's strikes in Germany and elsewhere.

Throughout the 1890s, *Die Gleichheit* was owned privately by the Dietz publishing company, as the SPD refused to finance, or even subsidise, it. Despite this, the paper clearly identified itself with the party, and with the politics of the party's left.

The paper's circulation grew rapidly: from 2,000 in 1891 to 11,000 in 1903/4 to 125,000 in 1914. The major cause of the big rise after 1904 was that the SPD (by then in control of *Die Gleichheit*) began distributing the paper free to socialist women and to the wives of SPD men. Good quality printed material was important, since women were less likely than men to go to meetings. *Die Gleichheit* played a central role in organising the socialist women's movement, in shaping its politics, and in developing the theoretical and practical work of German social democracy on the issue of working-class women's emancipation.

Disagreement arose over the theoretical "weightiness" of *Die Gleichheit*, as some complained that it was not populist enough. Clara Zetkin, Ottilie Baader and others, though, defended the paper's approach. They argued that it was aimed at the "more advanced women comrades", and that recruitment should be achieved through pamphlets and organisational work. The socialist women's movement needed not just general propaganda; it also needed a journal that could develop theory and educate its activists.

If *Die Gleichheit* were to be "watered down", they argued, it become less effective as a tool for organisers. And it may not necessarily gain mass appeal. Socialist publications should not aim just for high circulation, but have a definite purpose:

"The characteristic standpoint, that of class struggle, must be keenly and unambiguously stressed in a magazine for the interests of proletarian women ... Education of proletarian women precisely for the class struggle... will also in future be the chief task of *Die Gleichheit*." (*Die Gleichheit* vol.11 no.1 1901)

In 1902, the SPD took ownership of *Die Gleichheit*, and the Party leadership, agreeing with the paper's critics, began to force changes. From January 1905, supplements were included "For our housewives" and "For our children". *Die Gleichheit*'s editors and activists must have felt gutted.

The Party campaigned for laws to protect women workers. In the 1880s and 1890s, it repeatedly called for the appointment of female factory inspectors. In 1895, the new draft Civil Code included a section on family law that legislated power within the family to the husband and discriminated against unmarried mothers and their children. The SPD almost alone in the Reichstag opposed these new laws, whilst the socialist women mobilised actively against them.

The Party first advocated votes for women following its 1891 congress. In 1894, the SPD introduced a bill for women's suffrage to the Reichstag, and the socialist women held rallies to support the bill in Berlin and other major cities. The bill was defeated, but campaigning continued.

In 1898, *Die Gleichheit* began a regular column on women's suffrage. The women published several pamphlets and booklets, and articles in socialist papers. Clara Zetkin's pamphlet *The Question of Women's Suffrage*, published in 1907, was translated into Russian, English, Polish and French.

Outside Germany, socialist movements were not always so firm on this issue. Austrian socialists did not include women in their campaign to extend the franchise. British and Belgian socialist women welcomed votes for women with property as a positive, but inadequate, reform. Zetkin, though, argued that the vote for propertied women was not an extension of rights to women as women, but the extension of rights to the whole of the propertied classes, whether men or women. It was not a "first step" for women, but a "final step" for owners of property, strengthening their political power over workers.

The German women took the initiative in building international links between socialist women. At the International Socialist Congress in 1896 in London, women delegates met, and resolved to establish regular correspondence. But it was a further 11 years before the first official international congress of socialist women took place. It was held in 1907 in Stuttgart, convened by Clara Zetkin; 59 women from 15 countries attended.

The second international socialist women's congress, in 1910 in Copenhagen, resolved to hold an annual International Women's Day. But that's another story.

One of the most vocal women in German social democracy — and one of the leaders and greatest theorists of its revolutionary wing — was Rosa Luxemburg. She avoided involvement in the women's movement.

Luxemburg's biographer Nettl offers this explanation:

"Rosa Luxemburg was not interested in any high-principled campaign for women's rights — unlike her friend Clara Zetkin. Like anti-semitism, the inferior status of women was a social feature which would be eliminated only by the advent of socialism; in the meantime there was no point in making any special issue of it."

What Luxemburg omits is that the inferior status of women also holds back the fight for socialism. Like anti-semitism, sexism divided the workers' movement: it also impaired the confidence and material capability of women to become involved in the workers' movement.

By 1914, the SPD had 174,754 women members — 16.1% of the Party total. The crucial factor in their success was that they devised and carried out a specific strategy for working-class women. This could not come just from theory, but needed a day-to-day involvement in the lives and struggles of working-class women.

There was another crucial factor: the "target audience" should not be treated as a stage army. The movement involved women as activists, not as passive consumers. The debate over the nature of *Die Gleichheit* and the commitment to women's political education showed that leading socialist women such as Clara Zetkin were committed to building a movement of educated, skilled women, who were well-versed in socialist theory and able to speak confidently and contribute assertively to debate.

What is often seen as one issue — referred to at the time as the "woman question" — actually developed quite differently among women of different classes.

Women of the new capitalist class had a sharp experience of sexist discrimination, living alongside men of their own class who had achieved many of the political, educational and economic rights that they were still, as women, denied. These were women who did not share all the privileges of aristocratic women; but who (unlike working-class women) saw all the discrimination they faced originating from their sex, rather than their class.

The bourgeois women's movement came together as a loose federation in the League of German Women's Associations (Bund Deutsche Frauenvereine), founded in 1894. Its radical wing, represented in the 1890s by the "left liberal" Women's Welfare Association (Verein Frauenwohl), wanted to work with the socialist women.

Socialists disagreed about whether to work with the bourgeois women's movement. Clara Zetkin opposed cross-class collaboration, and this view predominated among the socialist women.

Why? Socialists believed that women's oppression was rooted in class structure. Capitalism has a drive to exploit labour as cheaply as possible, and a trend to shift production to the factory while social reproduction (taking care of workers, rearing children) remains within the home. Capitalism had not invented women's oppression, but had made its own "woman question" from sexual oppression inherited from previous class societies.

At the founding congress of the Second International in 1889, Clara Zetkin argued that, under capitalism, woman was enslaved to man, as the worker was to capital. Economic independence would enable working-class women to play their part in class struggle, but, without pressing the struggle forward to socialism, this would only replace slavery to a man with slavery to an employer. So the key to achieving women's emancipation was a fundamental change in property relations — production had to be owned and controlled collectively, the household economy had to be socialised to free women from the domestic burden. The socialist programme for women's liberation had to be a programme for the abolition of class society.

Zetkin's stance was also influenced by the Marxist argument for working-class political independence. As socialism had to be an act of self-emancipation, the working class could rely only on itself. However progressive a section of the capitalist class may be, it would still defend its own interests by defending capitalism.

Unless it acts independently, the working class is likely to be politically dominated by any section of the ruling class with which it collaborates. Eleanor Marx argued that "whenever working women meet together with bourgeois, it is the former who come under the influence of the latter".

Within the socialist women's movement, Lily Braun campaigned for co-operation with bourgeois feminists. She argued that "there are some modes of oppression which all women suffer, regardless of their class, and therefore that some collaboration with women not in the party was desirable".

Jean Quataert has written extensively about the German socialist women's movement. She agues that Lily Braun "symbolized their feminist consciousness" and that "In Zetkin's victory, class loyalty triumphed over sex identity." Quataert labels the German socialist women "reluctant feminists", and pursues a constant theme of a conflict of priority for working-class women between class and gender interests.

But does this conflict of interests really exist? Take a practical example. When working-class women fight for higher wages for women workers, there is no apparent conflict between class and sex interests. A woman capitalist, though, may wish to see women's pay reach equality with men's, but her class interests will oppose wage rises for workers. It is bourgeois women (and, in some ways, working-class men) who face a conflict.

But socialist women did face difficulties. Conflicts arose over the relative priority of issues; arguments in the party over its support for women's emancipation; and hostility from many socialist men toward the involvement and demands of their women comrades.

Socialist women consistently argued that women's involvement strengthened the workers' movement, and that women's oppression served the interests of the ruling class. In the working-class movement, women demanded that men put their class interests before their sex interests.

In 1896, Clara Zetkin presented the report on the "woman question" to SPD congress. The bourgeois women's movement, she argued, was engaged in a struggle against the men of its own class. Working-class women, on the other hand, were fighting alongside working-class men for socialism.

For Zetkin, working-class women's interests lay in overthrowing class society. The interests of women of the capitalist class, though, lay in preserving class divisions, albeit in a less sexist form. Working-class women were fighting a class struggle, and bourgeois women were on the other side.

A simplistic reading of this argument might infer that Zetkin exonerated working-class men from any part in oppressing women. But she recognised and fiercely opposed the sexist behaviour of working-class — and some socialist — men. Neither did she believe that only working-class women suffered oppression as women.

Zetkin's critics have argued that her policy led to missed opportunities. They urged co-operation with bourgeois feminists in, for example, the 1896 garment workers' strike.

Some bourgeois women did genuinely support the strikers' demands. But their agenda was that of "social reformers": they wanted to improve the lot of the most exploited workers in order to dampen class conflict. But socialist women sought to heighten the strikers' class consciousness. How could they inspire working women to fight against capitalism if they were in alliance with a section of their exploiters? With women who supported the wage-slavery system under which they were exploited?

On one major issue of class interests and of the real living conditions of working women, the bourgeois and socialist women took opposing stances. The SPD proposed several measures for legislation to protect women workers — for example, barring women's work around the time of childbirth. Even "progressive" bourgeois parties, such as the Centre Party, failed to support them.

Bourgeois feminists wanted the law to be "sex-blind", not to interfere in women's "right to work". They believed that working was better than not working because it freed women from domestic slavery. However, for working-class women, industrial labour was not a means of "getting out of the house" but an economic necessity — they needed to earn wages in order to survive. Neither did it necessarily free women from domestic slavery — usually, it just added to it.

The bourgeois women's attitude flowed from their privileged class position. They were not economically conscripted into the sort of dangerous, exhausting, unpleasant, unrewarding jobs that working-class women were. Their main concern was to escape boredom and frustration, rather than financial survival.

For socialists, women's entry into the industrial workforce was progressive, but full emancipation had to mean more than being exploited in the same conditions as male workers. The appalling condition in which many women worked, including during pregnancy, did not represent liberation: it represented suffering and enslavement at the hands of capitalism.

Even where socialist and bourgeois women agreed on demands, their respective priorities were very different. The SPD women called for various measures concerning women at work: the need for female factory inspectors; equal pay for equal work; the abolition of the system of domestic servants. There were further demands relating to women as mothers: support for women absent from work after childbirth; and removal of discrimination against unmarried mothers and their children.

Bourgeois feminists concentrated forcefully on "equal rights" issues, such as property rights. Before 1908, German law held that a woman needed her husband's permission to work outside the home; that she had to turn over to him all her property and income; and that she was under the legal guardianship of her father, then her husband.

Engels argued that, for the working class, the demand for "equal rights" had two possible meanings. It could be an expression of outrage at social inequality, and thus an articulation of revolutionary instinct. And it could be a means to mobilise people to demand the equality which capitalism promises, but only socialism can deliver. He concluded that "In both cases the real content of the proletarian demand for equality is the demand for the abolition of classes."

Engels warned that if it is not understood in this class context, "equal rights" becomes an illusion, even a prejudice.

Jean Quataert argues that "Socialist women became reluctant... feminists in their effort to balance the alternating pulls on working-class women's identity", and that "German socialist women were reluctant feminists because most of them regarded the feminist cause as a secondary concern overshadowed by the larger task of the class struggle." The suggestion is that their commitment to women's liberation was less genuine and enthusiastic than that of bourgeois feminists.

The socialist women were committed to ending class exploitation, private ownership, and all forms of inequality. The bourgeois feminists may have advocated women's equality, but they defended the class system which condemned millions of women to exploitation and oppression. It is hard to imagine an easy co-operation between socialist women and a movement which shared no other aspect of their political beliefs or aspirations.

After Bismarck's Anti-Socialist Law lapsed in 1890, laws remained which restricted women's political activity. The 1851 Prussian Association Law banned women from membership of political organisations, and from organising politically.

The application of the law varied between different states, but, throughout Germany, women's political activity was severely curtailed. In general, women were not allowed to attend any meeting at which public affairs were discussed. In 1886, Emma Ihrer was fined 60 Marks for discussing "unacceptable" topics, such as working women's wages and female suffrage.

Women were forced to get around these laws. In many cases, organising distinctly as women could achieve this, albeit temporarily. In some places, working-class women found it possible legally to take part in women-only meetings. Working women's associations survived (although not without harassment) until 1893, when the police disbanded them.

From 1900, some states relaxed the implementation of the Association Law. In 1902, the Prussian Secretary of State ruled that women could now attend political meetings alongside men — on condition that they sat separately, and did not clap or boo!

This signalled the beginning of moves within the SPD to reduce the organisational independence of the socialist women's movement.

In 1908, the Association Law was repealed, and the SPD set about completely integrating the women's organisation into the Party's structures. The Party Executive: dissolved all separate women's organisation; removed any independence from the Women's Bureau and subordinated it to the Party Executive; and assumed for itself control over agitation among women. The Women's Bureau was eventually to be dissolved in 1912, and the biannual Women's Conference was postponed in 1910 and subsequently abolished.

One seat on the Party Executive was to be reserved for a woman: Luise Zietz was appointed. At the time, she supported special women's organisations, regardless of the Association Law. Once on the Executive, however, she argued for full integration.

Ironically, in the same year (1907) that the German SPD abandoned the system of women organisers (Vertrauenspersonen), considering it no longer necessary after the law change, Austrian socialist women introduced the system. It proved a tremendous success: by 1910, the Austrian socialist party had 15,000 women members.

Clara Zetkin believed that the abolition of the Association Law did not abolish the need for some autonomy for socialist women. In 1908, she called for the retention of women-only groups for education and agitation. Five years later, Zetkin continued to argue that "If the women of the people are to be won for socialism then we need in part special ways, means and methods ... whose driving and executive forces are predominantly women."

The SPD integrated the women's organisation into party structures in the name of class unity. But some women felt that the opposite was true. Fride Wulff argued that relations between men and women in the SPD worsened following integration.

One result of integration was a new division of labour within the SPD. Women came to dominate work on welfare issues, especially child labour committees, and were kept out of positions of responsibility and authority on other matters. The evidence suggests strongly that formal equality and integration masked actual disunity.

When the National Executive refused to organise a women's congress in 1910, many women wrote to *Die Gleichheit* in protest. For these women, one of the roles of the women's section was to articulate the demands of women within the Party, and to do so against Party leaders if necessary.

In 1981, the Socialist Workers Party's founder Tony Cliff addressed the issue of the German socialist women's organisation: "If Zetkin opposed the ghettoisation of women workers both industrially and politically, why then did she build a separate socialist women's organisation? The reason was quite simple. The law did not allow women to join any political party in the greater part of the Reich until 1908. To circumvent the law Zetkin and her friends had to adopt very awkward measures."

But even when the Law was scrapped, the socialist women tenaciously defended their women's structures against the Party bureaucracy's attempts to dismantle them. The women clearly believed that these structures would continue to benefit their participation in the socialist movement, even when the legal necessity to organise distinctly no longer applied.

We can only speculate as to the course the women might have taken had they not faced these legal restrictions. But the benefits of special women's organisation. for both working-class women and for the workers' movement as a whole, go beyond the need to accommodate to repressive laws.

Cliff argued that only the Association Law caused women to organise distinctly. Does this mean that the law was the only obstacle to women's equal participation in the struggle for socialism?

The experience when such laws were not in force shows that simply the legal right to organise politically alongside men does not guarantee that women participate in equal numbers or on an equal basis with men. For example, in 1914 the French Socialist Party's membership of over 90,000 included fewer than 1,000 women.

In some cases, blame for the low level of women's participation rests with the anti-feminism of the policy and leadership of socialist parties. This was a factor in both France and England at this time. But in the German SPD, there was at least a theoretical commitment to women's equality. So, what further obstacles existed?

1. Socialists could not expect their own movement to be immune from the prejudices and gender socialisation of society as a whole: this socialisation discouraged working-class women from having the confidence or aspirations to be politically active.

2. Capitalist economic relations assign women an exhausting, time-consuming "double burden" of waged work and domestic labour.

3. Women also occupied a weaker position in the labour market. Women generally stayed in a particular job for a shorter time than men, which may have discouraged them from involvement in political or trade union organisation.

4. Women's limited education opportunities hit their ability and confidence to become active.

5. Discrimination in political rights — for example, the vote — served to assert that "public life" or politics was not a sphere for women.

6. Women's position as "the slave of the man" restricted a woman's ability to make her own independent decision to become involved in socialist activity. Even many socialist men discouraged their wives and daughters from becoming politically involved.

Women argued that, because of all these obstacles, it would be absurd for the Party to adopt a "sex-blind" formal equality in the Party's structures. This would do nothing to challenge inequalities; instead, it would mask them.

These women's experience points to two good reasons to see women's self-organisation as an appropriate strategy. First, the women's structure achieved obvious success in organising women in the fight for socialism. Second, it generated strategies for the SPD as a whole to take up the challenge of involving, recruiting and representing working-class women.

Clara Zetkin complained that: "In theory comrades have equal rights, but in practice the male comrades have the same philistine pigtail hanging down the back of their necks as do the best-wigged petty bourgeois." Others complained that capable women were obstructed; that women's criticism of the Party leadership or of male chauvinism in the Party was often put down in a sexist manner; and that male socialists used sarcasm and ridicule to undermine women.

For women on the Party's left wing, it seemed that just as the Party bureaucracy's reformist practice was increasingly at odds with its public, revolutionary rhetoric, so socialist men did not live up to their formal support for women's equality. Many socialist men acted as patriarchs within their own families, discouraging their wives and daughters from working outside the home.

Around the turn of the century, conflict intensified between the revolutionary and revisionist wings of the SPD. From 1897, Eduard Bernstein advanced theories that some basic elements of Marxism were no longer valid. He rejected the idea that capitalism contains contradictions that sow the seeds of its own demise. Bernstein also refuted the centrality of class struggle; he argued that revolution was not necessary for socialism, that gradual reforms of capitalism would be sufficient. Under this theory, the SPD's role would be as a propagandist electoral machine, not as a revolutionary, political leadership of working-class struggle.

The SPD left, which included Rosa Luxemburg and Clara Zetkin, strongly opposed this "revisionist" move. The revolutionary wing took up the issue of Party democracy and the dangers of growing bureaucratisation. Even before the revisionist tendency came to dominate German social democracy, the Party became increasingly bureaucratic; and while the SPD remained revolutionary in theory, it became increasingly reformist in practice. Sexist behaviour in the SPD took place in this political context. It was used by the right wing as a weapon against left-wing women.

The women's movement, though by no means politically uniform, was aligned with the SPD left. When the Party leadership supported Luise Zietz rather than Clara Zetkin for the new women's seat on the Party Executive in 1908, it was a political choice for an accommodating moderate over a vociferous revolutionary.

Tony Cliff puts together an argument which begins with support for Zetkin's stance against collaboration with bourgeois feminists, and concludes by denying any benefit from special women's organisation. Cliff argues that capitalist economic development simultaneously unites and divides workers — that while it creates a working class that is increasingly cohesive, it also sets up barriers between workers on the basis of (among others) sex and nationality.

Cliff cites Lenin's argument against the Bund, the Jewish socialist organisation in Russia. The Bund advocated that, due to the antisemitism experienced by Jewish workers, they should organise into a separate party, which would then have federal links with non-Jewish socialists. Lenin argued that this would divide and weaken the workers' movement.

But the German socialist women never put forward a policy such as the Bund's. Cliff does not draw any distinction between two quite different policies: on the one hand, a separate socialist women's organisation; on the other, distinct structures for women within the socialist movement.

Cliff also argues that "The relations between different sections of the proletariat are such that the weaker sections are helped very much by the stronger when there is a general upturn, while they are badly damaged during a downturn." Cliff seems to conclude that socialists should concentrate on "stronger sections", hoping this will develop the weaker sections in a "trickle-down" way.

Marx advocated working-class struggle to win legal reforms, welcoming the Ten Hours Bill in Britain in 1847. One reason for fighting for the "political economy of the working class" was that law reforms could advance the whole of the working class, whereas struggle in individual workplaces could benefit stronger sections but leave weaker sections still weak.

Weaker groups of workers may well benefit from the success of stronger groups, but it is also the case that strengthening the weaker sections benefits the movement as a whole. Not only do working-class women benefit from the struggles of working-class men, working-class men also benefit from the strong organisation of working-class women.

Cliff then claims that: "The higher the level of class struggle, the more accentuated are the differences between the level of consciousness and organisation of different sections of the class." He uses a low level of women's organisation as a measure of how advanced working class struggle is! He comes dangerously close to suggesting that working-class women have little contribution to make to the struggle for socialism.

Stronger sections of the working class may perceive their advantages over weaker sections to be privileges that they should defend. For example, male workers who followed Lassalle's policies saw women's entry into the workforce as a threat to their wages and status as men. There are many other examples, for instance "craftism" in the trades unions.

One more point about the "strong" and the "weak". From the Matchwomen to the Grunwick strikers, women workers have continually proved themselves to be stronger than expected. Write off women workers as a "weak section of the working class" and you risk under-estimating a source of great power.

If the working class is divided, if there are "stronger" and "weaker" sections, the question for socialists is: do we accept this as inevitable, or do we make efforts to redress this? And if working-class women, in struggling for their emancipation, build a socialist women's movement, how should a socialist party respond? By joining that movement and attempting to build and influence it? Or by arguing that it should give up any autonomy and liquidate itself into the general working-class movement?

Does women's self-organisation divide the workers' movement? Do supporters of self-organisation believe that the fight for women's liberation is a fight for women to wage alone? In both cases, no.

Although the German socialist women were continually frustrated by the attitudes of men in the labour movement, Zetkin did not believe that working-class women could or should achieve liberation by themselves. She saw women's liberation being achieved through socialism, and socialism being achieved through the united action of the working class. The purpose of building women's organisations was to bring women into a united workers' movement, not to separate women off into a liberation struggle apart from socialist men.

All working-class people share a common interest in overthrowing capitalism and achieving socialism. Nevertheless, some groups enjoy a degree of privilege within capitalism. Their benefits may be marginal and short-term, but could still influence working-class men's attitudes to the struggles of working-class women. Will they — as socialists would wish — oppose sexism and unite with women in the pursuit of a common goal? Or will they defend their privileges as men at the expense of working-class unity and struggle? Women's organisation, and socialists' input, can be crucial in determining the answer.

Socialists need to devise and implement a strategy to relate to working-class women. For the German socialist women, this included having definite bodies and individuals with a remit to organise work amongst women. Together with women's political education, publications, congresses and international work, this strategy reaped great rewards.

But this is not just about structural set-ups, nor about recruiting female foot-soldiers. The struggle for socialism is about self-activity. So we need a women's movement based on rank-and-file activism. This is why Clara Zetkin insisted that *Die Gleichheit* was not simply for entertainment: the paper was a tool for activists — an agitator, educator and organiser.

The German socialist women stand out from other women's movements in one crucial way. In other cases, cross-class women's movements did not have a mass appeal among working-class women, and came to represent the interests and aspirations of middle-class women.

Even if this is not an argument for an entirely separate movement for working-class women, it is a convincing case for orienting any existing women's movement toward alliance with the workers' movement. Without this, a women's movement can easily swing politically to the right.

But the decisive point is this. Even if women of all classes experience oppression as women, the form and degree of this oppression — and its solution — is so different that any commonality of women's interests does not override class differences.

The German experience also shows that the fortunes of the women's movement are closely linked to the fortunes of working-class struggle. Within a mass workers' party, political conflicts affect, and find expression in, the women's section.

In German social democracy, the left showed genuine support to the aspirations of working-class women, while the revisionist right did not. Worse, the Party's bureaucracy was prepared to crush the women's organisation as part of its battle against the left and against the rank and file.

To fulfil the potential of women's contribution to its struggles, the labour movement must make itself accessible to women. It should purge sexism within its own ranks, and fight effectively for working-class women's interests. The experience of the German socialist women's movement shows that organisational autonomy for women contributes greatly to making the socialist movement accessible and attractive to women. It helped develop women's confidence and skills, and enabled them to put their demands onto the agenda of the socialist struggle.

WOMEN IN THE RUSSIAN REVOLUTION

BY JAYNE EVANS

In the latter half of the 19th century the Russian economy was still primarily rural. But cities were growing rapidly, industrial production was increasing and the old feudal social order, built around the autocratic regime of the Tsar, was being shaken.

A woman's lot in life varied according to which class she belonged to. For peasant women, and the increasing numbers of urban working-class women, life meant poverty, endless labour and abuse. Upper-class women might sometimes own property, but all women were considered subordinate and expected to be submissive to men. Divorce was difficult. In law women were considered to be worth half of a man. However, circles of better-off and middle-class women saw themselves as part of the intelligentsia and were challenging their alloted role. Some were involved in radical politics.

In the 1860s the Russian intelligentsia's movement for political change began in earnest. One part of it were "the Populists" or "Narodniks". They were utopian socialist, their socialism based on an ideal of communal land ownership organised by the village. Maybe as many as a quarter of the people involved in different groups and networks were women. Like many utopian socialists in Europe, the Russians considered an improvement in the lot of women to be a measure of general social progress.

One wing of the Narodniks used terror tactics to avenge the brutal actions of the autocratic Russian state and, so they believed, to spark an uprising. Women were involved in these actions.

Many middle-class and intelligentsia women (liberal as well as populist) sought access to education and, through writings and petitions, won segregated schools for women, some university courses and a medical school. This was Russia's first feminist movement. By 1900 the Russian Women's Mutual Philanthropic Society had been established. Even though it campaigned for peaceful reform their organisation was still illegal. They also did charity work — "helping" the poor and prostitutes.

Russian Marxism, as it developed after the early 1880s, was in good part based on a rejection of the tactics and politics of the Narodniks. They wanted to build an organisation that would base itself on the growing working class, against the bourgeoisie.

Small numbers of women were involved in the first Marxist circles from the beginning — Vera Zasulich is the most well known. The first congress of the Russian Social and Democratic Labour Party was held in 1898.

In 1900 Lenin (living and working abroad) helped set up the newspaper *Iskra* (Spark) to help organise the new organisation, and to relate to a growing workers' movement. The second congress of the party was held in 1903 in Brussels and

London. There the party separated into two factions — the Bolshevik (majority) faction and the Menshevik (minority) faction. Between 1906 and 1912 the factions were again united in a single organisation.

The whole period from the late 1870s to 1900s was a time of awakening of class consciousness among the Russian proletariat, of strikes and walk-outs. Women were a large part of the new proletariat.

Women workers took an active part in the worker revolts at the Krenholm factory in 1872 and at the Lazeryev textile factory in Moscow in 1874. They were involved in an 1878 strike at the New Cotton-Spinning Plant in Petrograd. They led a weavers' strike contingent in the workers' demonstration in Orekhovo-Zuyevo, during which factory buildings were wrecked. That action forced the Tsarist government to bring in legislation prohibiting night work for women and children (1885).

The new and intensified wave of worker disturbances in the mid- and late 1890s saw working women playing a role. The Marxist (from 1915 Bolshevik) Alexandra Kollontai described what these struggles meant for the woman worker:

"In these struggles as in all those that follow, the woman worker, oppressed, timid, without rights, straightens up to her full height and becomes equal as a fighter and comrade. This transformation takes place unconsciously, spontaneously, but it is important and significant.

"However, no sooner had the wave of bitter strike struggle passed... than the women were once again isolated from one another, still unconscious of the need for organisation."

Kollontai explained that, "In those years it was still unusual to find a woman worker in the illegal party organisations. The life led by six million proletarian women in Russia at the beginning of the 20th century was still too dark. A 12-hour, or at best an 11-hour working day, a starvation wage of 12-15 roubles a month, accommodation in overcrowded barracks, the absence of any form of assistance from the state or society in case of illness, pregnancy or unemployment, the impossibility of organising self-help as the Tsarist government savagely persecuted any attempts at organisation by the workers — these were the conditions surrounding the woman worker."

This in part explains why the women involved in building the underground socialist movement in Russia were people like Kollontai, often from middle class, wealthy, even aristocratic backgrounds who had to leave their parental homes, break with their past and even leave children to the care of others, to become fighters against social injustice.

Between January 1905 and the autumn of 1906 Russia was consumed by mass strikes and protests. As the strike wave spread many women workers got involved. Women were at the front of the demonstrations on 9 January 1905 — Bloody Sunday — when 150,000 striking workers and their families marched through St Petersburg to deliver a petition to the Tsar only to be shot at and ridden down by the army.

The upheavals saw the first soviets — self-organised democratic workers' decision making bodies. Delegates were elected from factories, workplaces and army barracks, and committees were set up to organise self defence, policing, militias, to make laws, and control production.

Those events turned many women into revolutionaries — teachers, school girls,

RECLAIM INTERNATIONAL WORKING WOMEN'S DAY!

On 28 February 1909, socialist women in the USA held their first national Women's Day, staging marches and meetings across America to demand political rights for working women. The next year, Clara Zetkin proposed to the International Congress of Socialist Women that one day each year be marked as a Working Women's Day. Socialists in all countries should hold big events, involving men and women, demanding improvements in the lives of working women. In 1911, more than a million women and men marched and rallied in Denmark, Germany, Switzerland and Austria.

On 25 March 1911, less than a week after that first International Women's Day, more than 140 workers died in the Triangle Fire in New York. Mostly young Jewish and Italian immigrant women, they burned to death when the Triangle Shirtwaist Company factory where they worked caught fire. They died because working conditions were terrible and safety measures lacking, because capitalists pocket the profit they make from women's labour rather than spending it on civilised working conditions. Capitalism killed them.

Millions of women still work in sweatshops and other jobs with low pay and poor conditions — as well as unpaid in the home. There is not a country in the world where women have full equality with men.

Since socialist women founded International Women's Day, it has been adopted by non-socialist feminists, governments and even the United Nations. It is now more likely to be marked by an aromatherapy open day than by a march for women's rights. We should return to the original purpose of the Day: to mobilise support for working-class women's demands, and to celebrate the contribution that women make to the struggle for human liberation.

students, and the intelligentsia. These are some of the stories of those times.

• Two non-party students assisted a Bolshevik urban guerrilla group prepare an armed uprising in Kronstadt. Both were shot, one while pregnant.

• The Bolshevik Olga Genkina was torn to pieces by the Black Hundreds (Tsarist-loyal terrorists) who found her carrying a suitcase with propaganda and arms.

• Yakoleva was pulled out of a May Day demo and jumped on by armed men — she recovered from her injuries and remained a key organiser and fighter.

• Rozaliya Zalkind served as an *Iskra* agent — she directed the Moscow uprising of December 1905, in charge of deploying armoured trolley cars on the streets. In 1917 she once again organised armoured cars and divisions of men and women.

Bolshevik women were organisers and teachers. They were couriers and smugglers. They distributed literature and weapons, organised and spoke at meetings. In 1905 these women learned administrative and military skills which would be used again in 1917.

Children of underground couples had to be taught how to conceal publications and leaflets. One daughter of a Bolshevik agent wondered why her mother gained and lost weight when travelling from flat to flat and was confused as to why her parents always told her to tell the truth when they were forever lying about what they were doing!

The revolution of 1905 awoke all layers of society, industrial workers, but also middle-class people who wanted to reform the Tsarist autocracy. The bourgeois women's movement which had gone into decline in the 1890s revived. The Women's Progressive Party and the Alliance for Female Equality were established by middle-class "bourgeois" feminists. Women workers were also thinking about their political rights as well as making economic demands. Kollontai explains:

"That women workers were no longer indifferent to their lack of rights is also shown by the fact that, of the 40,000 signatures on petitions addressed to the First and Second State Dumas [undemocratic Parliaments set up by the Tsar] demanding that electoral rights be extended to women, a large majority were those of women workers."

The collection of signatures was organised by the Alliance for Female Equality and other bourgeois women's organisations but was conducted at plants and factories. The woman worker still naively accepted the hand held out to her by bourgeois feminists. These "suffragettes" — like their equivalents elsewhere in Europe — turned to working women to get support and to organise them into purely feminine, supposedly non-class, but essentially bourgeois alliances — to win rights for bourgeois women! However, a healthy class instinct and a deep mistrust of the "fine ladies" saved women workers from being attracted to this kind of feminism and prevented long-term or stable fraternisation with bourgeois suffragettes.

For the women of the working class, exhausted by the burden of intolerable working conditions and the material insecurity of their families, immediate demands were different: a shorter working day, higher pay, a more humane attitude on the part of the factory administration, less police surveillance, more freedom of action.

The bourgeois feminists were particularly disappointed by their initiative among domestic servants — they organised meetings of domestic servants in St Petersburg and Moscow in 1905. The domestic servants eagerly responded to this call to "organise" and turned up in large numbers. However, when the Alliance for Female Equality tried to organise them according to their own tastes, i.e. to set up an idyllic, mixed alliance between lady employers and domestic employees, the domestic servants organised their own special trade unions.

The domestic servants' movement overflowed the boundaries predetermined for it by the feminists. During 1905 domestic servants organised direct action, even in the most remote regions of Russia. This took the form either of mass strike action, or of street demonstrations. The strikes involved cooks, laundresses and maids; there were strikes according to profession, and strikes that united all domestic servants. The demands made by the domestic servants were usually limited to an eight-hour working day, a minimum wage, more tolerable living conditions (a separate room), polite treatment by the employer, etc.

For the first time in Russia, the Russian peasant woman took to protest. The end of 1904 and the whole of 1905 is a period of continuous "petticoat rebellions".

The peasant women attacked military and police headquarters where the army recruits [involved in a war with Japan] were stationed, seized their menfolk and took them home. Armed with rakes, pitchforks and brooms, peasant women drove the armed guards from the villages. They were protesting against the intolerable burden of war. They were arrested, tried and given severe punishments.

In this protest, as elsewhere, a defence of peasant (class) interests and of purely "female" interests are closely interwoven.

Marxist socialists in Europe had a policy of organising working-class women. Most Social Democratic parties stood for such things as maternity services as well as public housing and health. They argued that overthrowing capitalism would bring the liberation of women. But Alexandra Kollontai thought that the Russian Social Democrats were making little practical effort to draw in working women—who made up 20-30% of the working class and suffered the worst conditions.

Kollontai was based in St Petersburg during the events of 1905 and at that time she fought unsuccessfully to get the local party to set up a special bureau to organise work among working-class women. In 1906 she travelled to Germany to attend meetings of the German Social Democratic Party (SPD) who were organising impressive work amongst working-class women.

When Kollontai returned to St Petersburg she organised lectures and discussion groups among women. Her work was not hindered by the party but they did not help it either. In 1907 Clara Zetkin, a key leader of the German working-class women's movement, called for the establishment of women's bureaus in each national party. The International approved but the Russian Social Democratic Party thought the idea too close to "bourgeois feminism". Instead, they believed that women would be freed by revolution and that it was more important to win the whole working class to socialism.

In 1907 Kollontai, together with Klavdia Nikolaeva, set up the Society for the Mutual Help of Working Women as a counter-weight to the liberal feminist women's clubs of the time. The experiment was short-lived.

Kollontai was in favour of a separate organisation to help involve working-class women in struggle but one that would not make alliances with bourgeois feminists. She thought that if women's issues were ignored, women would not join class struggle. She began to develop her political ideas. All socialists at the time used Frederick Engels' *The Family, Private Property and the State* (1984) and

August Bebel's *Women and Socialism* (1879) as their basis for thinking about "the Woman Question".

Engels had said the destruction of private property would remove the basis for male supremacy and the economic foundations of the family. Women would work as equals and the care and education of children would become a public matter. Private relationships would be based on "sex love".

Women and Socialism sketched out a socialist society where there would be public provision of health, pregnancy and childbirth institutions, and public education. Under socialism the family would continue but parents, free of economic worries, would have leisure time to devote to their children.

In *The social basis of the woman question* (1909) Kollontai argued that women must throw off the contemporary, obsolete, coercive form of family — the bourgeois family — in order to be free. But she attacked the idea of "free love". That was, said Kollontai, a luxury that working-class women could not obtain under capitalism. For instance, poorly paid working-class women could not deal with childcare responsibility if they had to bring up their children alone. The economic situation first had to change— there needed to be public provision of health and education and an end to exploitation at work. Kollontai proposed a radical and new idea about childrearing (one put into practice by socialist-Zionists in the kibbutz movement). She said bringing up children shouldn't be the job of an amateur; children should be educated by trained people who had a collective, socialist outlook.

Kollontai believed that only under socialism could any woman have truly free relationships. Until men and women were "re-educated" by new social conditions men would treat women as possessions and women would subordinate themselves. Kollontai thought that marriage destroyed individuality, particularly for women; married couples thought they possessed each other— they gave up their privacy.

But Kollontai also thought a new morality should develop before the revolution, particularly between socialists. Relations should be based on solidarity and equality. For Kollontai, developing this ideology was part of the class struggle. The "new woman" (a common feminist idea of the time) was constantly leaving men because she made demands they couldn't meet — she demanded to be free. She saw this new woman as both a sign of a new morality (a reflection of changing social conditions) and something that would be fully realised under socialism.

The mainstream feminist Women's Mutual Society organised a congress in 1908. Kollontai organised delegate elections from the textile workers and the trade union bureau to attend the event. At the congress the workers' group had 45 out of 1,000 delegates, the rest were middle-class professionals. The group argued that only class struggle could free women, and put resolutions calling for legal and political equality and social reform. On the last day the workers' group walked out.

Many of the Bolshevik women took a different tack to Kollontai and developed their own ways of work among women, often in opposition to Kollontai and Zetkin. They were able to organise and agitate effectively despite the lack of women in the organisation. (At the 1912 organisation only 13 out of 394 present were women. From 1898-1912 only five out of 69 central committee members were women). It is true that "women's work" was not considered a priority and there was a tendency to brand any women's work as feminism. On the other hand Lenin and later Yakov Sverdlov were two prominent and consistent allies of the organising among working-class women.

The Bolshevik Konkordia Samoilova organised an illegal meeting on International Women's Day in February 1913. Its subject was factory conditions, prostitution, peasant life and the 1905 revolution. After the meeting several women were arrested. Samoilova suggested a special paper for proletarian women was produced in response to letters they had received following the meeting and the arrests. It was called *Rabotnitsa* [*The Woman Worker*].

The editorial board consisted of three groups of women. In St. Petersburg the group included Anna Elizarova (Lenin's sister) and her associates; in Cracow, Nadezhda Krupskaya and Lilina Zinoviev; in Paris, Ludmila Stul and Inessa Armand. Armand drew up the outline of contents — theoretical articles would be written by her and Stil. Krupskaya said some articles should be of a general nature and not just focused on women. There would be agitational articles and letters.

Rabotnitsa was largely driven by Inessa Armand. Amazingly, the authorities in St Petersburg granted permission for publication of the paper. They hoped to publish in time for International Women's Day 1914. However, the state raided the women's organisations in the run-up to the day and key women were arrested. But *Rabotnitsa* came out, largely due to the efforts of Elizarova who had evaded arrest. She managed to produce seven issues of the paper (print run 20,000, each 16 pages long). It was sold in factories for four or five kopeks a copy. Armand wasn't happy with *Rabotnitsa*. It wasn't as theoretical as she wanted. It included letters and poetry. It had printed a Menshevik account of Women's Day. These disagreements were a reflection of political tensions between the émigré leadership and comrades in Russia.

When Krupskaya proved unable to bring the editorial board under the control of the foreign editors she stopped contributing. However, *Rabotnitsa* won many women workers over to the Bolsheviks; it broke down stereotypes about the "backwardness" of women workers; and, despite a lack of enthusiasm among male Bolsheviks, it broke down the idea that "women's work" was separatism or a feminist threat.

In most books Inessa Armand is treated in a derogatory way; she is called "Lenin's book carrier and Girl Friday". Yet she carried out important party work, and was one of the people who represented the party internationally. Armand was nominated by the party central committee in late May/June 1914 to be the Bolshevik delegate to the International Women's Secretariat. She was the Bolshevik representative in European conferences. She was relied on to talk to wavering Bolsheviks. She translated and delivered party pronouncements.

On many occasions these assignments brought her into conflict with many of the leaders of European socialism. She was an organiser. She was entrusted with the reorganisation of the Paris emigré Bolshevik section. She intervened with the Ukrainian Social Democrats.

When the executive of the International Socialist Bureau (ISB) called a conference in Brussels on 16 July 1914 to bring together the two wings of Russian Social Democracy she was a key Bolshevik delegate. Talk of unity — and considerable pressure to bring it about — was overtaken by events.

When the First World War broke out, the Second International collapsed, as most socialists supported the defence of their "own" countries and got behind governments' war efforts. Later, anti-war socialist conferences were held.

In 1914 Inessa Armand fled to Bern in Switzerland. On 26 March 1915 a women's conference was held in Bern. The Bolsheviks wanted the conference to put out a revolutionary call — "turn the imperialist war into a civil war"— and to condemn the leaders of the Second International.

Clara Zetkin wanted to involve centrists and pacifists and called the conference in the name of the International Women's Secretariat so that it would be an official meeting. Armand tried to organise the election of Bolshevik sympathisers to the international delegations. On the day, 27 delegates from eight countries met and just five were Bolsheviks.

Zetkin put a conciliatory motion; the Bolsheviks put a separate one saying the only way to guarantee peace is through revolution. Armand spoke for the Bolsheviks. Zetkin wanted her to withdraw the motion to present unity. Armand refused.

However, the Bolsheviks agreed to vote for Zetkin's motion if the Bolsheviks' motion was printed and recorded. Despite these efforts Clara Zetkin was dismissed from her post at the German socialist women's paper *Die Gleichheit*. The German SPD leadership were supporting the war. Zetkin was arrested.

Despite its conciliatory tone, this was the first international conference of socialists to oppose the war. It was an important step towards building working-class opposition to the war.

On 5 September 1915 the (anti-war) Zimmerwald Conference was held and the Bolsheviks' tough anti-war stance was pushed forward further.

Meanwhile, Armand was in France working in the Confédération Générale du Travail (CGT) and the French Section of the Workers' International (SFIO) for the anti-war position.

During 1917 the Bolsheviks were agitating for an end to the war, explaining why it was an imperialist war. Some patriotic pro-war people set up the League of Personal Example and began to organise highly disciplined shock battalions or death battalions to fight which could, they hoped, convince people to die for their country. It was in this atmosphere that Maria Bochkareva was charged to create the 1st Russian Women's Battalion of Death in May 1917. It fought in the "June offensive" on the Russian western front.

Maria Bochkareva organised her battalion with strict moral discipline and all the punishment and humiliation you would usually find in the army. Bolshevik agitators spread dissent in the battalion, arguing for a soldiers' committee or for it to be disbanded. Kollontai reports that there were no proletarian women in the battalion, just peasants, wealthy women and students.

Liberal feminists lavished praise on The Battalion of Death. Anna Shabanova hosted a meeting with speakers Emmeline Pankhurst and Bochkareva in June 1917. Pankhurst had been sent by Lloyd George to bolster the pro-victory spirit of women.

Another women's battalion — the 1st Petrograd Women's Battalion — was ordered to defend the Winter Palace against the Bolshevik-led insurrection on 25 October, but only 135 of the battalion were sent, and in the event even they refused to fight, saying their role was to fight at the front.

Undoubtedly the Bolsheviks, despite the failings of earlier years, were the best propagandists and organisers of proletarian women in 1917. Everywhere women were being elected to serve on committees. The liberal feminists renewed their agitation for the vote. Proletarian women too wanted suffrage. The Bolsheviks had to compete (to a certain extent, they were forced to compete) for the political allegiance of proletarian women.

By 1917 a third of Petrograd's factory workers were women; half of the workers in the chemical industry were women; two-thirds of the workers in food, textiles and tailoring were women.

The February revolution — beginning in earnest on International Women's Day (though there had been a build-up of strikes in the period before) — saw the establishment of a Provisional Government. The government did not and would not either end the war or solve the food crisis. However, after political parties were made legal, the Bolsheviks attemped to use the democratic opening to build their organisation.

At the 13 March party congress, Vera Slutskaya proposed that a bureau of women workers be set up and the paper *Rabotnitsa* was revived. In April and May agitational bureaus, commissions and groups were set up across Petrograd with a teaching cadre at the centre.

Eventually women's commissions were established at the district party level. Clubs and trade union activities were used to draw non-party working women into party activities.

Throughout 1917 the women's organisations worked to build a conference of women workers. This conference of 500 delegates representing around 80,000 women workers would meet shortly before the October revolution.

The Bolsheviks intervened in the liberal feminist meetings. When the feminists held an "All Russian Women's Congress" in Moscow a delegation headed by Inessa Armand repeated their earlier tactics of 1908 and walked out after reading political statements.

One example of a Bolshevik campaign was agitation among laundry workers who worked 13 or 14 hours a day. The Bolsheviks called for public laundries, better conditions and the setting up of a library. The laundry workers went on strike and raised the political demands put forward by the Bolsheviks — opposition to the war and "all power to the soviets".

The Bolshevik women agitated among soldiers' wives for more money, but unlike the liberal feminists they did not appeal to the Provisional Government. They called on the Petrograd Soviet to force through the measure.

Alexandra Kollontai organised a committee for the distribution of funds to soldiers' wives and a union of soldiers' wives was set up in many cities. Kollontai also called on soldiers' wives to send delegates to the soviets.

On 10 May *Rabotnitsa* reappeared. It was to be published several times a month and gained a circulation of 40-50,000. It agitated about the war, high prices and labour conditions.

In the industrial-military centres of the city the work was supplemented by other campaigns. Nadezhda Krupskaya and Zhenya Egrova worked in the Vyborg district, Slutskaya on Vasilevsky Island, Ludmila Stul on Kronstadt naval base and Anna Itkina in the Narva district. Inessa Armand travelled up to Moscow and organised around the journal *The life of the woman worker*.

Rabotnitsa relied on women workers' support. A group of women workers had agreed to support *Rabotnitsa* even before it was produced — pledging three days' pay. Money for copies sold was taken to the office where paper distribution and meetings were arranged; *Rabotnitsa's* supporters also wrote articles for the paper. It was more than a journal— it was used to train agitators. In May a 10,000 strong meeting was held at the Cimizelli circus.

The *Rabotnitsa* group in Petrograd would write copy in the morning and then travel to the factories in the afternoon.

After a series of mass demonstrations in July there was a clampdown on political activity. Bolshevik women were even attacked by their workmates and denounced as spies. But the tide would turn. A mass meeting in August called for the release of Kollontai from prison.

In the last couple of weeks before October, hundreds of thousands of workers took and consolidated their control of their factories and barracks. Peasant revolts swept the countryside. Two-thirds of factories had committees. In Petrograd 1,200 deputies were elected to the soviet. In March and April there had been 700 soviets with 200,000 delegates across Russia. By October there were 1,400 soviets. The Provisional Government had no grip on events — their declarations and orders were met with indifference. Mass meetings of thousands took place in halls, workplaces and streets — people were involved in controlling their own lives.

Kollontai wrote: "Stick to your revolutionary posts, women workers. All our strength, all our energy, all our thoughts must be given to strengthening the power of the revolutionary democracy, the power of the soviets. The place of working class women in these great days of the first proletarian revolution is amongst the courageous fighters for revolutionary ideals."

The Bolsheviks were opposed to the politics of the women's battalions — the prosecution of the imperialist war. But they were not against women fighting. Bolshevik women were involved in armed actions and in street fighting.

Women took part in the Red Guard. Several women were involved in the Petrograd soviet's Military Revolutionary Committee. Women were involved at every level.

Lenin's verdict: "In Petrograd, here in Moscow, in cities and industrial centres, and out in the country, proletarian women have stood the test magnificently in the revolution. Without them we should not have won, or just barely won."

The Bolshevik women, who had years of experience in making propaganda and agitation, fought off accusations of "feminine weakness" to take a full part in making propaganda in the civil war which followed the 1917 Russian revolution.

Alexandra Kollontai travelled to the front taking instructions from the centre, and making speeches. Nadezhda Krupskaya did the same on the Agitational Boat. For all of the Bolsheviks the civil war was a continuation of the revolution.

In May 1918 the first Russian women's conference was held. Just 130 delegates attended. But a Women's National Congress held in November 1918 saw 1,147 women attending.

In her speech, Inessa Armand condemned the double burden of women — factory work and household slavery. The revolution had destroyed the capitalist economy, she said, now it was time to break up the household economy and free women to participate in party, soviet and other activities. This could be done by setting up communal nurseries, kindergartens, laundries and kitchens. She called for delegate-based meetings of women in all areas.

The main demands of Bolshevik women delegates were adopted. Prominent among these demands was protection and provision for motherhood. The first concern was to maintain and rebuild children's homes in Petrograd and Moscow; they were to be converted into "angel factories", homes for mothers and children. They decided to take control of all the existing crèches, consultation centres and children's homes (very few in number) that had been founded before the revolution by charitable organisations.

Inessa Armand was made chair of a new Central Commission for agitation and propaganda amongst working women and was to be assisted by Kollontai and Konkordia Samoilova. The job was to raise political consciousness through meetings, schools and propaganda circles; they would encourage party membership and involvement in soviets, factory committees and the trade unions; they would set up communal facilities.

During the first months of soviet power decrees were passed aimed at improving the material conditions of life for working-class women. One decree ordered all lying-in hospitals and all centres, clinics and institutes of gynaecology and midwifery be transferred to the Department for the Protection of Mother and Child. Medical services for expectant mothers would be organised on the basis of three new principles:

1. that medical assistance be available to all mothers in need;

2. that doctors be paid a state salary, thus abolishing the advantages enjoyed by more prosperous women able to pay the doctor for services; and

3. that expectant and nursing mothers, particularly the poor, be protected against becoming "sacrifices to science", being practised upon by unskilled midwives and medical students.

The decree also replaced one-year midwifery courses with two-year courses.

The next step was to bring together in one state organisation all of the institutions caring for mother and child in the pre- and post-natal periods, and all institutions involved in child care, from children's homes to village crèches. The same decree ordered the creation of a model Palace of Motherhood, the conversion of all the lying-in hospitals and children's homes in Moscow and Petrograd into one general institution known as "The Moscow Children's Institute" and "The Petrograd Children's Institute". Children's homes were renamed young children's palaces.

The revolution released a burst of optimism and aspiration for a society built on socialist principles. Discussions raged among young people on sexual relations, child rearing and the nature of the family in the transition to socialism. Creative energy gripped cultural fields as well. Priorities and tasks changed to reflect the widely held view that the family would soon wither away.

A month after the revolution, two decrees established civil marriage and allowed for divorce at the request of either partner. The divorce rate soared in the following period.

A complete Code on Marriage, the Family and Guardianship, ratified in October 1918, swept away centuries of patriarchal and ecclesiastical law, and established a new doctrine based on individual rights and the equality of the sexes. The Bolsheviks also abolished all laws against homosexual acts and other consensual sexual activity.

"Soviet legislation bases itself on the following principle: It declares the absolute non-interference of the state and society into sexual matters, so long as nobody is injured, and no one's interests are encroached upon."

The new Family Code was drafted by a committee headed by AG Goikhbarg, a former Menshevik law professor. They described their code as "not socialist legislation, but legislation of the transitional time," just as the Soviet state itself, as the dictatorship of the proletariat, was a preparatory regime transitional from capitalism to socialism.

The code eliminated the distinction between "legitimate" and "illegitimate" children. Now women could claim child support from men to whom they were not married. The code established the right of all children to parental support until the age of 18 and the right of each spouse to his or her own property.

In implementing the code judges were usually biased in favour of women and children on the grounds that establishing support for the child took priority over protecting the financial interests of any man.

Goikhbarg later said: "They screamed at us: 'Registration of marriage, formal marriage, what kind of socialism is this?'" His argument was that civil marriage registration was a means to an end, crucial to furthering the struggle against the medieval grip of the Russian Orthodox church. Without civil marriage, the population would resort to religious ceremonies [e.g., to establish "security" for their children] and the church would flourish.

Women's commissions were established for propaganda and agitation and in 1919 the Zhenotdel (Women's Department) was set up, with Inessa Armand as director.

The Zhenotdel sent teams of women into the religious areas of eastern Russia, where Muslim, Christian, Jewish and Buddhist women were subjected to strict codes regulating sexual behaviour, unknown in the rest of Russia. The most severe codes were those imposed in the Muslim areas where women had no status other than as pleasure giver, servant, housekeeper and child bearer. Their isolation and untouchability was bolstered by the veil, the most extreme form being the paranja, a heavy horse hair garment worn from nose to floor.

Armand and Kollontai brought some of these women to Moscow conferences; once there they would tear off their face coverings as a sign of emancipation.

Teams were sent out into mountain villages to meet and talk to women. When women came to the cities of the east they organised secret meetings in bath houses and women's clubs.

In Baku the women's club had thousands of members; it became a school and social centre. Women agitators toured central Asia showing films of a Muslim heroine refusing to marry an old man who had bought her.

Some men reacted with savage violence. In Baku the women were attacked with dogs and boiling water as they left the club. Some women were mutilated and many murdered — 300 in 1929.

Despite the dangers hundreds of women from these areas volunteered to be translators, assistants, agitators. Each May Day and on International Women's Day thousands of women would assemble and tear off their veils.

The Zhenotdel was to provide child and orphan care, school service and inspection, food distribution, preventative medicine and public health, anti prostitution campaigns, education, and housing.

In all her tasks Inessa Armand was diligent. She was the contact for the maternity and infancy sections of the Commissariat for Health, for the Education Commission and for the struggle to end women being forced into prostitution; she organised courses and produced literature. She organised women to work in factories, join the medical corps, and fight in the Red Army.

In 1920, when the civil war was coming to an end, the Zhenotdel organised delegate meetings. Those meetings discussed establishing crèches, literacy and educational courses and participation in soviets. Crèches were set up in factories; canteens to provide meals; communal kitchens and dining rooms. The Zhenotdel set up communal laundries. Nurseries and kindergartens were created and 1,500 mother and child centres set up. The Zhenotdel popularised and administered these communal services.

By April 1919 *Pravda* had a regular women worker page, as did local papers.

In 1920 a new paper *Kommunista* was produced, aimed at more literate women and covering more theoretical issues. Again, Armand was central to the work, working 14-16 hours a day. She was involved in the final preparation for the first international conference of communist women scheduled for July 1920. An international section was to be established which Inessa was to head but she died, exhausted and malnourished, before the conference took place.

Alexandra Kollontai became head of the Zhenotdel for the next two years.

All this good work, like much else that was inspiring about the Russian Revolution, was smashed up by the counter-revolution led by Joseph Stalin — the effect of the isolation of the revolution, the civil war and terrible economic hardship.

Some women, such as Alexandra Kollontai, accommodated themselves to the Stalinist regime. Others supported the groups which opposed Stalin.

The new order — from the mid/late 1920s onwards — reversed the huge progress that had been made for example bringing in control over divorce and abortion, reinforcing the old traditional family unit.

We have a great deal to learn from the Bolshevik women and the events of the Russian revolution.

These women were agitators, organisers and educators equal to the Bolshevik men. They faced sexism, opposition and indifference from many members of the Bolshevik party. Even women such as Krupskaya and Armand didn't take a vocal or prominent role at party conferences and, given the central political roles they undertook, the responsibilities they held, and in all areas of party work, this is difficult to understand and impossible to accept.

Women still constituted a small proportion of the Bolshevik party membership. Lenin wrote about how the party was refusing to take the work of organising working class women seriously and instead saw it as the work of women comrades exclusively.

But the Bolshevik women fought against all pressures. Why would they not? They were dedicated revolutionaries. The stories of many of their lives are now forgotten, as are the sacrifices and heroism of the thousands of working class women in the Russian revolution. But by building a movement based on the lessons of their struggles, we will ensure that working-class women liberate themselves and help overthrow capitalism.

WHAT WE STAND FOR

Whilst we fight for the politics of women's liberation within the labour and student movements here and now, we recognise that women's oppression is rooted in class society. We believe that the emancipation of women can only happen with the emancipation of humanity as a whole through the socialist transformation of society through class struggle.

What do we mean by socialism? In capitalism the means of producing wealth exist on a huge scale, but they are owned by, and operated in the interests of, a small minority. Socialism means the people who produce the wealth, the working class, taking power and taking control of these means of production, making them collective property and allowing society's wealth to be used for the good of all.

The working class is the vast majority, a very broad group of people, immensely diverse, but united by their dependency on waged labour. Millions of working-class people, both men and women, cannot find sufficient waged labour, even though they depend on it. They may rely on informal trading, the resources of working-class household, and plots of land, informal work or kinship groups. Men and women have this dependent relationship to waged labour but it is differentiated by women's role in childbearing; the ability to stitch together childcare; and the gendered division of labour that structures the availability, price and type of wage labour men and women do.

A politically conscious working class could overthrow the bosses and start a process of abolishing classes. Advanced science and technology could finally combine with conscious, democratic planning to meet rational human goals, whether dragging down carbon emissions to avoid dangerous climate change or abolishing institutionalised forms of oppression.

Overthrowing class exploitation is a necessary building block, but not enough in itself to abolish oppression. Socialism will not immediately end all oppression, but the roots of oppression lie in class society — by overthrowing class society and cutting the roots of oppression we can create the conditions for liberation. In a society based on democracy and solidarity it will be possible to work to end all forms of oppression and exploitation.

What could this offer women? It's impossible to work out a blueprint for a socialist future — a revolution would release forces, tendencies and human potential in ways we can't predict. We get glimpses of how society could work during big struggles under capitalism — for example, during the 1984-85 miners' strike women who began organising kitchens and food distribution soon proved themselves to be formidable public speakers and inspirational campaigners. A lot of the old sexist attitudes were pushed back.

One idea would be to reorganise domestic work on a collective basis: communal kitchens, housekeeping services, flexible and free childcare and so on. This would not only remove the burden of housework for women but free personal relationships from economic ties and end domestic dependency. Women's vulnerability would reduce and their status would rise. Using science and technology to make life better, rather than to make profits, would also give us more free time to pursue our interests and develop ourselves. In the course of all of these processes, people would change.

We could raise a new generation of human beings free from at least the worst of "the old crap", allowing new relations between men and women and even challenging the gender structures inherited from capitalism.

But class society, not least the capitalist form of class society, has carried with it, and sometimes sharpened oppressive social-cultural customs and practices. Women, racialised groups, sexual minorities and so on bear the brunt of oppressive cultural norms. The family has been a key instrument for capitalist accumulation (helping to depress wages and ensure the reproduction of workers' labour power); a means by which working-class families can survive (pooling resources and providing emotional sustenance); and the site of a lot of oppression (the gender division of labour, gender stereotypes, domestic violence). Women's oppression is complex — bound up in both class and cultural realities.

Our concept that women's oppression is complex and integrated with class relations helps us to avoid "dual systems" theories that see women's oppression as existing in parallel with capitalism or any other economic system. We have, in the history of our tendency, not used the term "patriarchy" to describe the structures of women's oppression. However, Carmen Basant has here looked at the development of feminist struggle in India, argues that "patriarchy" may be a useful way of describing how the broadly greater status men have is fused with capitalist social relations.

We don't see women's oppression as separate from, or subordinate to, class oppression. In *Marxism and the Oppression of Women*, Lise Vogel is critical of much of the socialist tradition, including socialists of the Second International, for seeing a separation between class and women's oppression and crudely bolting the so-called "woman question" onto class analysis. She says this led some in the Second International to deny the "critical significance" of women's liberation or conceive of it as a reformist ambition that "scarcely differed, at a practical level, from bourgeois nationalism or liberal feminism".

Whatever we make of Vogel's critique, the legacy of Stalinism, the conservative inclinations of union bureaucracies, and gender inequality within the labour market itself are some of the factors which have allowed a concept of class struggle which is divorced from the goals of women's liberation to persist in the labour movement.

The main problem is that unions do not or only half-heartedly fight on issues that are most relevant to women workers — low pay, insecure employment, lack

TAFADZWA CHOTO (1975-)

Is a member of the national coordinating committee of the International Socialist Organisation (ISO), in Zimbabwe. She became active in the women's movement in the early 1990s. She was politicised after witnessing a woman at the University of Zimbabwe being stripped of her skirt. Tafadzwa Choto became active in the ISO at the time of the riots in Harare, sparked by police killing three civilians when chasing some thieves. In 2001, at a May Day Rally in Harare, she was savagely beaten by Robert Mugabe's thugs. In 2012, Tafadzwa Choto and five other ISO members were imprisoned and convicted for watching a video about the Egyptian uprising, but released after international protests.

support with caring responsibilities.

In addition, although major unions have equalities structures and comprehensive formal equality policy, sexism in the labour movement has continued to thrive. Women trade union activists taking a strong stance often face sexism from both bosses and co-workers (including within their union), especially in industries which remain male-dominated.

Some sections of the labour movement are dominated by a particular concept of class struggle and militancy which is expressed as (and reduced to) machoistic posturing and explicitly denigrates feminist struggle. We say militancy of class-conscious confrontation with our bosses can and should include militant struggle over women's oppression.

Recently, the way in which sections of the revolutionary left relate to liberation and equality has also come under the spotlight. There have long been problems with some on the left either side-lining liberation struggles, or using them opportunistically. This was brought into sharper focus by the mishandling and minimising of serious allegations of sexism and violence against women by the two biggest groups on the British left, the Socialist Workers' Party and the Socialist Party. The issue here was not so much that these organisations put "class struggle" above the fight for women's liberation, but that they subordinated both to something that is, for them, more important: self-preservation. These failings link to what we in Workers' Liberty have previously described as "apparatus Marxism". That is, putting perceived organisational advantage above political

WHAT DO WE STAND FOR?

• Tax the rich! Rebuild the welfare state and NHS — cuts, closures and privatisations often affect women most acutely
• A living wage for all workers; decent, affordable housing; and a comprehensive benefits and welfare system
• Against sexism in the labour movement — the demands of women workers should be central to trade union struggles
• For free, flexible and good quality childcare
• Against religious fundamentalisms. No repression and persecution of women in the name of religion!
• For free movement of workers and refugees world wide — no borders!
• For sexual freedom and liberation for lesbian, gay, bisexual and trans* people
• Against sexism in our schools, colleges, universities and workplaces
• Against all forms of violence against women: sexual harassment, rape, domestic violence and abuse. Increase public funds to provide adequate support services for women
• For solidarity with women workers worldwide; against sweatshop labour
• Solidarity with sex workers, full decriminalisation, legal recognition as workers.
• Against sexist images, against censorship
• For safe, legal and free abortion on demand and an end to the social pressures and stigmatisation around women's reproductive choices

principles, in these cases the principles of transparent and democratic functioning, accountability of leaders, and women's rights. In the case of the Socialist Party, the influence of the machoistic culture of the labour movement also played a role.

For a revolutionary concept of class conflict that integrates class and women's liberation, Vogel suggests we follow a similar approach to that used by the Russian revolutionary leader Vladimir Lenin. Vogel praises Lenin for what she describes as his insistence that there is a "material core embedded in all social relations, even those involving women, the family, and sexuality". Lenin saw the structures of women's oppression as part of the reality that revolutionary politics must address. Vogel quotes Lenin: "No matter how much democracy there is under capitalism, the woman remains a domestic slave... The right of divorce, as all other democratic rights ... is conditional, restricted, formal, narrow".

Lenin pointed out that the situation for women in Russia was integral to the structures of Russian class society, for example, their "domestic slavery". But he did not advocate postponing struggles for equality until a revolutionary overthrow

WHO WE ARE

Workers' Liberty's socialist feminist work arises out of our active trade unionism and student activism or through getting involved in broader feminist campaigns.

In 1979 we began Women's Fightback with the hope of attracting women active in the labour movement, and socialist feminists who were thinking about how to fight the Thatcher government. Around that time a layer of left women joined Labour to pursue that political fight and many were active in Labour Party women's sections. The first conference of Women's Fightback was sponsored by a wide range of labour and women's organisations and drew 500 women. Women's Fightback went on to produce a monthly newspaper (with the same name) and played a role in Women Against Pit Closures. Unfortunately, the defeats of the 1980s meant that struggle in both the labour and women's movements declined and Women's Fightback became a smaller campaign. Workers' Liberty continued to discuss and intervene in feminist campaigns where they existed.

When, at the turn of the 21st century, feminist ideas and activism revived among a layer of young women, that revival was reflected in the student movement. In 2006 women members of the left student group, Education Not for Sale launched Feminist Fightback, in which we were involved. Feminist Fightback continues to organise as a left feminist collective.

In 2007 we restarted Women's Fightback as a bi-monthly paper.

The renewal of global anti-capitalist struggle has, with breaks, dominated left-wing politics since the turn of the century. In this context, we continue to be active with other socialist and anti-capitalist feminist activists, especially in National Campaign Against Fees and Cuts Women. We also run discussion and reading groups, have a Women's Fightback blog and paper and have organised two successful socialist feminist conferences.

OUR BLOG: WOMENSFIGHTBACK.WORDPRESS.COM

of those class structures. He campaigned for women's divorce rights, for example. Nor did he assume that women's situation would necessarily improve after the Russian revolution of 1917 without deliberate, conscious effort. The practical measures implemented after 1917 were an attempt to address this situation within a process of the revolutionary transformation of society.

WORKERS' LIBERTY AND CLASS-STRUGGLE FEMINISM

Drawing on older socialist traditions Workers' Liberty argues that gender oppression becomes imbricated in social relations through complex historical processes. Second, that women's historically subordinated position in "domestic life" is key to our oppression along with the sharp separation under capitalism between domestic households and economic production, the private and the public.

Capitalists are also able to exploit divisions of ethnicity, culture, nation etc. On the one hand they provide the basis for extra exploitation of some groups. On the other hand they undermine working-class solidarity and resistance. However, there remains a real basis for solidarity — the common experiences of capitalist exploitation. Class exploitation is not necessarily worse or more fundamental than other oppressions; but because class structures are bound up with nature, technology and how society's wealth is produced, these are a powerful force in shaping *all* social divisions and inequality.

The fight for equality and liberation is an inseparable part of our socialism. We do not tell women — or any oppressed group — to wait for the revolution for their liberation. Without the abolition of class exploitation, there can be no end to women's oppression. But without a mass movement of organised, mobilised women fighting against sexism and oppression and for liberation, there can be no socialist revolution. We recognise that a key task for socialist feminists today is to challenge sexism within our movement — this remains fundamental to transforming the labour movement and to supporting the struggles of working-class women on other issues.

KEY ASPECTS OF OUR SOCIALIST FEMINISM

Democracy

In many capitalist societies a limited amount of political democracy exists. But the majority of people have no meaningful say over how society is run. We want a much fuller democracy — a consistent democracy in every aspect of human life.

There can't be collective ownership and planning without democracy. Effective workers' struggle is impossible without democracy. The working class needs democratic rights (to organise, to strike, to demonstrate, to publish our ideas). Women are half of the world's population — our voices should be heard! True democracy needs women's involvement, and women need democracy if we are to change the systems and laws that discriminate against, and oppress, us — that also means democracy in our movements so that they fight for our rights too.

Internationalism

Women's oppression is global and so our response needs to be international. In many parts of the world millions of women continue to live without very basic rights: reproductive rights, the right to an education, to work, the right to divorce, and the right to live free from violence. But pretty much everywhere feminist ideas have taken some hold or had some impact. For us solidarity across borders, is at the heart of our socialist feminism.

Revolution

The key to a socialist feminist approach is looking at how women's subordination develops throughout history. Capitalism introduced a particular form of the mechanisms through which women are oppressed (such as the family) and it's important to understand these mechanisms if we're going to challenge them. History shows us that oppression is not an unchanging and unchallengeable fact of existence. It's not "human nature" or just about individual relations between men and women, although it is often embodied in them.

We think it's important to learn about and discuss history and ideas. We look at class and feminist movements of the past — not because we think there was ever a "golden age" but so that we can gain inspiration and learn the lessons from both strengths and flaws, victories and defeats. We want to think about how socialist feminism can help us understand the world today and how to fight in it.

We can make important gains under capitalism and should fight for these, but they're small steps, are insecure and need constantly defending. We don't think we can win full equality under capitalism because of the way women's oppression is woven into its functioning. Capitalism has no motivation to pay for the services and support needed to give women real choices about what we want to do. Even if we could win equality, it would be equality of exploitation which is not the kind of equality we want! That is why we want a revolution that will replace capitalism with socialism!

HOW CAN WE FIGHT FOR THESE IDEAS?

Working-class women cannot opt out of class struggle — so feminists cannot ignore the labour movement. Class struggle what we used to win the rights we have now (from equal pay legislation, to maternity leave, to even the right to vote) and class struggle will be fundamental to ensuring our rights are defended and extended.

Aside from needing defences against our bosses, women are half the workers' movement and we're entitled to demand that it fights for our rights and interests. As socialist feminists, we see our job as reorienting the labour movement towards a fight for women's rights, and the women's movement towards class struggle.

We want to transform the labour movement — including stamping out sexism. Our hopes for this lie with the rank-and-file members. We want ordinary union members to get organised. We don't just want more women in top union jobs, or gender-balanced committees — we want democratic unions that champion the fight for women's liberation. Women's organisation within our trade unions is central to making this happen: it makes it easier for women to get involved in the union, and ensures that women workers can raise issues relevant to us and demand action on those issues.

REVOLUTIONARY ORGANISATIONS

If we're going to end our exploitation and oppression we need to get organised — this is the role of the revolutionary organisation. It allows workers political and organisational independence from the ruling class. But, most important, ideological independence. Karl Marx said that the dominant ideas of any society are those belonging to and formulated by the ruling class. Against them, we need our own ideas and ability to learn from and analyse the world around us. We need to cut against the grain of the dominant ideas in society, and a big part of that is challenging the ideas around oppression and developing a programme for liberation. We take these ideas into the wider movement and fight for them, and reshape them based on that experience. Revolutionary organisations also serve as what Leon Trotsky called the "memory of the class", enabling us to learn, and never forget, the lessons of our movement's past.

Workers' Liberty wants to build a revolutionary "party", an organisation that has the active allegiance and political involvement of large sections of workers in their workplaces and in their communities. To build such an organisation it is necessary to have an organisation which is both active in struggles and developing ideas.

A NEW WOMEN'S MOVEMENT?

Women have never enjoyed equality — in pay, politics or society. Now, to pay for capitalism's crisis, we have been pushed back further, suffering disproportionately from cuts to jobs, health and welfare, and the growing strength of the reactionary right. In the UK we still provide the bulk of the domestic labour, not least in caring for the young, old and ill, left by the way-side by austerity. We face attacks on our reproductive rights, our sexual freedom and expression, and attacks on our bodies and minds through domestic violence and abuse and sexual violence. It's the same, and worse, for women the world over, hit by poverty, climate crisis and religious fundamentalisms.

Socialism can end women's oppression. But nothing is inevitable — socialist ideas give us the framework for creating a more equal and liberated society. But it's up to us to make it happen by fighting for these ideas. Organising to build a women's movement that can challenge and remake the attitudes of the labour movement to put liberation at the heart of our struggle is central to this.

In the past working-class women's movements have played a key role in the class struggle — challenging the labour movement and pushing it forward; developing ideas and theories about women's oppression and liberation; and ensuring socialist feminism takes up the issues which affect women's everyday lives.

As long as capitalism continues, as long as women's oppression continues to be maintained by and intrinsic to capitalism, women's movements will emerge again and again. We cannot, however, will them into existence. We can't predict how and when a movement could emerge and what form that might take. We do know that, throughout history, the fate of women's movements and the fate of working-class movements have been tied together. There will be no effective women's movement without connections to the labour movement — but equally there can be no revitalised workers' movement without women getting organised.

WOMEN AGAINST PIT CLOSURES

The miners' strike of 1984-85 was an all-out battle between workers and the Tory Government. And Women Against Pit Closures (WAPC) were on the front line of that battle. They organised food collections and distributions and raised funds for the strike. But they soon became much more than a support group, organising pickets, rallies and demonstrations, travelling around Britain and overseas for public speaking, often for the first time.

WAPC was a magnificent alliance between women in a whole range of tightly-knit working-class communities across Britain, and feminists. Socialist feminists were prominent in miners' support groups. The strike, and women's organising around it, took the politics of women's liberation — both at the level of political demands and ways of organising — into parts of the working class that it had never before reached.

The miners' strike was defeated after 12 months of hard-fought struggle. It is certain that the miners could not have fought so well or for so long without the strength of the women. Importantly, the miners, and the workers' movement, had to see women as strong, active, political people. Before the strike, the National Union of Mineworkers' newspaper had its own Page 3. Afterwards, while sexism was, of course, not eradicated, it would have been unthinkable for Page 3 to continue.

The women changed too. More women went on to further education, some relationships broke up — and perhaps others changed. Some women from mining communities continued their political involvement. One woman from South Yorkshire described it like this: "It was as though women had been asleep for hundreds of years. We awoke to a new awareness, a realisation of what we as women could do... Do you know, I believe we are part of history being made."

WAPC was just one example of the potential of struggle to create solidarity. During campaigns in the late 1990s, women from groups such as Women of the Waterfront (supporting the Liverpool Dockers), the Hillingdon Hospital strikers and the Magnet Women's Support Group became formidable public speakers and inspirational campaigners. The ruling class has to send its people to elocution lessons and finishing school to make them fit to perform in public. But our people — women from these struggles like Doreen McNally, Malkiat Bilku and Shirley Winter — are more than a match for any of them.

Working-class women have a vast store of talent, ignored and suppressed by capitalism, which bursts out when prompted by the demands of class struggle.